A PREACHER AMONG THE PROPHETS

GEORGE B. DUNCAN

HODDER AND STOUGHTON
LONDON   SYDNEY   AUCKLAND   TORONTO

British Library Cataloguing in Publication Data

Duncan, George
  A preacher among the prophets.
  1. Bible. O. T.   2. Prophets
  I. Title
  221.9′22   BS1198

  ISBN 0-340-26356-3

Printed in Great Britain for Hodder and Stoughton Limited, Mill Road, Dunton Green, Sevenoaks, Kent, by Richard Clay (The Chaucer Press) Limited, Bungay, Suffolk. Photoset by Rowland Phototypesetting Limited, Bury St Edmunds, Suffolk. Hodder and Stoughton Editorial Office: 47 Bedford Square, London WCIB 3DP.

A Preacher Among
The Prophets

Also by George B. Duncan

A Preacher's Life of Jesus

Dedicated
to my Friend and Brother in Christ
Donald Wellman
Senior Pastor of the First Church of the Nazarene,
Denver, Colorado, USA,
together with Pat, his wife, and Carol Witt,
his secretary who has greatly helped in
the preparation of this book for the press,
not forgetting
the other members of the staff and of the
congregation who welcomed myself and my wife
into the warmth of the fellowship we all share
in Christ.

'I thank my God upon every remembrance of you'

Phil. 1:3.

Verses by Amy Carmichael reproduced by the
kind permission of the Society for Promoting
Christian Knowledge.

Introduction

Throughout my ministry I have been fascinated by the lives and words of the men and women whose stories appear in the Old Testament. I suppose this may in part be due to the influence of Dr. Alexander Whyte, that greatest of all Scottish preachers, whose books of sermons on Bible characters gave me insights that I have never had before. There were indeed 'giants in those days'! What rugged, massive characters so many of them were, and yet what insights into the needs of the human hearts both of people and of nations. Their words were not simply concerned with foretelling, but rather with forthtelling God's word to His people. This basic relationship of life between sinful man and his Creator God was their constant theme: and as we study their words and their own characters we realise that basically neither man nor God has changed throughout the passing of the centuries. Compared with them, the ministries of our days seem insipid and anaemic. It may be that a study of the messages in this book of sermons delivered in many lands may help some of us face up to their challenge of man's need of being 'right with God'! Passionately concerned as so many of the prophets were with issues of social justice, nevertheless the main thrust of all they had to say dealt with this! At the same time we find to our great comfort that they were men of 'like passions' as ourselves! It is my earnest prayer and hope that these messages may bring comfort as well as challenge to those who read these sermons, as so many in the mercy of God found as they heard them preached!

Contents

1.	Moses: The Call to Involvement	11
2.	Moses: When the Load is too Heavy	19
3.	Samuel: What Can Happen in Old Age?	26
4.	Samuel: The Sin of Prayerlessness	37
5.	Nathan: The Coronation of the King	46
6.	The Old Prophet: A Peril of Spiritual Maturity	53
7.	Elijah: The Dark Hours of the Soul	62
8.	Elisha: A Miracle of Recovery	73
9.	Elisha: The Sin of Silence	80
10.	Nehemiah: The Way People Talk About God's Work	90
11.	God's Remedy for Man's Loneliness	99
12.	The Garden of the Soul	107
13.	Isaiah: Among the Hills	115
14.	Jeremiah: In the Hands of the Potter	124
15.	Jeremiah: The Unexpected Place of Blessing	131
16.	Daniel: The Hidden Secrets of True Greatness	137
17.	Hosea: The Discipline of Withdrawal	145
18.	Joel: Back Moves	152
19.	Zechariah: The Servant of God and the Spirit of God	160
20.	Malachi: Life's Refining Fires	167

1

MOSES: THE CALL TO INVOLVEMENT

'Come now therefore and I will send thee' (Exodus 3.10).

Sometimes when you and I look at a great life mightily used by God, our thoughts are thoughts of envy, of admiration mixed with a sense of hopelessness that such greatness is not for us. If, however, we trace such greatness back to its origins, we might learn some lessons and discover some facts that might bring the whole matter surprisingly within range and within reach.

The story of the call of Moses is a story that does just that for us, illustrating the principle that the New Testament states, namely, that God uses 'the weak things of the world to confound the mighty, the things that are not, to bring to nought the things that are'. There are four words that seem to sum up what happened in the life of Moses which jerked him up out of obscurity into prominence, out of ordinariness into greatness, making him a figure of destiny not only in the life of his nation but in the whole history of the entire world, who would wield an influence that has scarcely been matched by any other man. I want us to note in the first place –

HIS CONTENTMENT. In Exodus 2.21 we read: 'And Moses was content to dwell with the man and kept his flocks.' Here was a man who had at one time held high hopes of serving God and his generation in a big way, a man who had indeed made bold if rash attempts to do so, only to find that his attempts had failed and had ended in disaster! Now he was a man who had settled down and accepted that such greatness is not for him. He had fled from the scene, he had lost a position of potential influence and power, and was now a shepherd looking after sheep, a man who had married and had settled down in the middle years of his life, and who was now quite content that things should be that way. So he was to live for forty years, and our story opens in the eightieth year of his life. The Bible stresses the fact of his contentment: 'He was content to dwell with the man and kept his flocks.'

Two factors contributed to his contentment. The first was *the passing of the years*. How long ago it was, and yet, sometimes it must have seemed as if it was but yesterday, that he had seen the oppression of his people in Egypt, and in a burst of anger he intervened and killed the oppressor, only to find that he had then to flee the land. It seemed like yesterday that he had dreamed his dreams of the deliverance he would bring to his people, and then suddenly disaster had struck! But it was not yesterday, it was all in the distant past, forty years had gone by! He was no longer the man he had been then. Great achievements were for the young, not for men of his age. For forty years he had lived with his sheep, his dreams, his thoughts and his memories. Yes, the passing of the years had contributed to his contentment. The time for greatness was gone. He had dreamed and had failed and his failure must be final. During those long forty years there had come no summons from his people, no call from His God. He had been forgotten by both and must content himself with his quiet and pleasant lot!

I often wonder whether there are other people like Moses. They live contentedly, they have settled down to trivial living but with memories of dreams they used to dream of attempting great things for God, and of achieving great things for God; memories of rash and sometimes crude efforts to bring God's saving grace to bear upon the lives of others, attempts that had been designed to achieve so much, but had ended in seemingly total failure. Since then many years have passed, years that have been void of any real spiritual significance.

Another factor that may have contributed to the contentment of Moses was not only the passing of the years but *the pattern of his life*. We are told in Exodus 3.1: 'Now Moses kept the flock of Jethro his father-in-law.' In those far off days as a young prince in the court of Pharaoh, with the influence he could have wielded in court circles, something could have been done to bring deliverance to his oppressed people – as a prince, yes, but as shepherd, no, a thousand times no! Shepherds did not deliver nations, they looked after sheep! He had better be satisfied with the job he was doing and had been doing for the last forty years. The time for dreams, for achievement, was past and gone! He was a shepherd and that was that!

Have not many men and women felt the same way, have they not been in a similar situation? What is your task right now? Is it as far removed from significant living as was the task of Moses looking after the sheep? Are you a secretary in an office? Are you a nurse busy looking after the sick in a hospital? Are you a shop-assistant spending your time behind the counter? Are you a teacher, a mother? Are you working in a factory as an engineer? Are you unemployed, retired? Do you think along the lines that Moses must surely have thought again and again, what has what I am doing, and have been doing for so long, to do with spiritual greatness and achievement? Is there something in common between you and this man who lived so long ago? Let us then follow Moses in the next step. I want you to share with him and with me –

HIS AMAZEMENT! Something happened one day that shattered the even tenor of his life. This man who had settled down to a life of obscurity was suddenly startled, and stabbed awake. What happened that day changed everything for him, and the events of another similar day can still change the whole course of the life that God is still waiting and longing to use!

I want us to note *What was seen by him*. There was a vision that came to him; we read about it in Exodus 3.2. He saw a bush and we are told: 'The bush burned with fire, and the bush was not consumed!' that Moses 'turned aside to see the sight'. What did the sight of the burning bush signify to Moses? Did it speak to him of his people, that nation which was still suffering in the fires of persecution, that people whose sufferings and whose need he had almost forgotten? They were still his people, they were still God's chosen people, and while he was living a cosy and comfortable and contented life, they were still in the furnace of affliction. The need was still there for a deliverer; nobody else had appeared! What was he doing living so contentedly while his people were suffering at the hands of their oppressors?

Or did the bush speak to him of his person? It was just a common bush, an ordinary bush, a bush that nobody would have noticed or thought important. But this bush was alight and aflame with the presence of God. It was transformed. It was a sight so wonderful that it demanded investigation and explanation. Did this sight suggest that even a shepherd could become a deliverer? The bush was a miracle; could God work a miracle in his life? At that moment when he turned aside to look, we are told that 'the angel of the Lord appeared unto him'. God then was concerned with him, with Moses the reject, the failure, the shepherd, the older man; and the message that the vision brought home to him was that whatever he might think about himself, God thought differently!

The other thing that contributed to his amazement was not what was seen by him, but also *what was said to him*; and what God had to say to him was something that staggered him! The story was told to him bluntly of the desperate plight of God's people, and the forces that oppressed them and made their lives a misery, and then came the unbelievable word of challenge to him, 'I have seen the affliction of my people, I have heard their cry, I know their sorrows, I am come down to deliver them, come now therefore and I will send **thee** that **thou** mayest bring forth my people out of Egypt!' What must have staggered Moses was the realisation that God wanted him, that his people needed him, and that God was going to send him back to do the very work that he had once dreamed of doing! At the very time when he thought he was on the shelf, he was to be the instrument in the hands of God to do one of the biggest jobs ever done by any man before or since. He was to find himself right in the centre of the stream of God's will for a vast multitude of people; the reject was required and wanted!

I believe that there are scores of Christians who today need to make a similar discovery, scores and scores of ordinary people doing ordinary jobs, people who have long since given up any idea of God ever doing anything of real significance through them in the lives of others. There are lives that have known failure into which God wants to bring success. There are older men and women who have been leaving far too much to the young, and God wants them to rise up, and do things that long ago they had once dreamed of doing; there are lives that have been marked by spiritual and moral tragedies, through which God still wants to bring about some of his greatest victories. Is this God's word to someone reading these lines, a word that tells you that God wants you still, that God needs you now?

We have thought of the Contentment of Moses, of the Amazement of Moses, now let us look at something he needed desperately, and that was –

HIS ENCOURAGEMENT. How wrong we can be if we are tempted to think that the lives which God uses have been the lives of men and women who have been confident in their own abilities. Nowhere is the reverse of this seen more clearly than in the call of Moses. Listen to *the protests he made*, protests so like our own, protests that kept on tumbling from his lips, for no sooner had God answered one, than Moses found another. 'Who am I that I should go?' Exodus 3.11. 'What shall I say?' Exodus 3.13. 'They will not believe me' Exodus 4.1. 'I am not eloquent' Exodus 4.10; and then the final way of escape, 'Send someone else' Exodus 4.13. There is something so very human about it all. The way he talked, seemed so out of keeping with the great work that God was going to do through him. It is fascinating to study our Bibles and find out how again and again this is the reaction of those whom God calls, whom God uses. It was so with Jeremiah – his protest was, 'I am a child . . . I cannot speak'. It was the same with Gideon: 'Who am I that I should save Israel . . . I am the least in my Father's house.'

When the call comes to us to bestir ourselves to move into action, to attempt something for God that seems utterly impossible, is our reaction not just the same? What, me?! 'I could never do that! I'm not the man! I'm not the person! I could never speak to anyone.' But the witness of both the Old and the New Testaments is to the fact that God still uses the weak things of the world to confound the mighty. When I look back to my own boyhood, I could never have imagined then that God would give me the privilege of doing all the things He has given me to do since then.

But in reply to the protests Moses made, we find *the promises he got*, and they combined to silence every argument he brought forward, and dispose of every excuse he made. The basic promise, which included all the others, was the promise which said, 'I will be with thee' Exodus 3.12, and again in Exodus 4.12, 'I will be with thy mouth'. If God was going to be with him, what could he lack? Nothing! The promises to Moses were few in comparison to those made to the Christians in the New Testament, but basically they, too, are wrapped up in one, 'Lo I am with you always.' This was the promise that sustained David Livingstone who, when facing danger and hostility and death itself, rested his heart on that word from God, adding that it is 'the word of a perfect gentleman of the most strict and sacred honour.' What more do we need than Christ, the Lord of glory, made real to us in our weakness, through the ministry of the indwelling Holy Spirit of God?

Is it any wonder then that we can conclude our study by noting finally –

HIS ACHIEVEMENT! The first thing to note is that what Moses now began to do was marked by *the authentic stamp of the presence of God*. 'I am too ordinary a person,' said

Moses, 'they will say "The Lord hath not appeared to thee.' The one great essential, both for leader and for those led, would be the conviction that God was in all they were doing and attempting to do. So God began right there with Moses, and said, 'What is that in thine hand? Throw it down', and when Moses obeyed, that shepherd's rod became a writhing serpent. The rod was the symbol of the work that he had been doing day after day. God in effect said to him, 'I want to touch your life with miracle, I want to demonstrate in your life a power which can only be explained in terms of My power.' I believe that this is God's method still. He wants to begin by touching your life with miracle, the ordinary life you live where you are right now. 'What is that in thine hand?' Is it a saucepan, a typewriter, a school book? 'Let me touch that with miracle, let me show the world that my power is at work in your life, that you are becoming the kind of person that only I can make you.'

The other thing to note was that Moses began to be caught up into *the majestic sweep of the purpose of God*. Here was a man looking after sheep and God wanted him to deliver a nation, and that nation one that would make its impact upon the whole world, that would play a decisive role in God's eternal plan of salvation for the whole world! Let us never forget that the will of God has both an individual and a universal content, and that the eternal and universal will of God has to be worked out through personal and individual obedience to the will of God. The Bible states quite clearly that 'God wills that **all** men should be saved' and to make that possible Christ 'gave His life a ransom for **all**'. And don't let any theological theory devalue the word 'all', twice repeated by Paul. God does not of course get His way in many lives, but His will is clearly stated. He waits for men and women in whose lives, and through whose lives, His will may be done! How many millions of Christians have prayed the prayer that Christ taught the children of God to pray, and have said, 'Thy will be done.' But these same Christians seem never to ask themselves what that will is, and by whom it is to be done! It is not a will of God to be done to us, to be endured by us.

17

Surely it is the great redemptive will of God to be done by us and through us in the lives of others. Moses was looking after sheep, and all the time God wanted him to deliver a nation. What are you doing, and what does God want you to do?

Those who have been to any of the crusades led by Dr. Billy Graham will be familiar with one phrase that he uses almost every time that he makes an appeal for commitment to Christ. He will say, 'I want you to get up out of your seats and come to the front.' It is the phrase 'I want you to get up out of your seats' that seems to me to be the modern equivalent of the challenge that came to Moses so many years ago. God wanted him to get up out of the comfortable life he had been living for so long and to get involved in the huge task of meeting the needs of a whole nation and leading them out of bondage into liberty. It is not a nation that God is concerned with today, it is the whole world, that world which begins at your front door and mine. God wants us who name the name of Christ to get involved, by our giving, by our praying, by our caring and by our sharing, so that the appalling needs of mankind may be met out of the wealth of the grace and mercy of God. To you and to me the word comes not from an American evangelist, but from God Himself, 'I want you to rise and get up out of your seats.' Will you do just that and do it now?

2

MOSES: WHEN THE LOAD IS TOO HEAVY

'They shall bear the burden with thee' (Exodus 18.22)

How amazingly up to date the Bible is in its message, and how amazingly unchanging are the pressures and problems that confront the people of God down the centuries. This eighteenth chapter in the book of Exodus recalls a story and a situation that took place thousands of years ago, and yet it might just as well have happened yesterday!

The incident poses a question that all Christians would do well to face and try to answer. The question is this – in the life and progress of the kingdom of God are we part of the burden of the work, or are we under the burden of the work? This needs to be faced individually and personally. I wonder what your answer would be. Do you add to the weight of the task or do you help with it? Let us examine this whole chapter of Exodus and see what light it has to throw upon the relevance and importance of facing and answering this particular question.

The setting of the text is the appointment of those who would 'bear the burden' with Moses as he tackled the task God had given him. We note –

THE LIMITS THAT SHOULD BE SENSED IN THE WORK OF GOD. Someone once asked, which is the greater man; the man who can do the work of ten men, or who can get ten men to do the work? Whichever is the greater, and possibly the latter is, it is obvious that there is a limit to what one man can do. This is what Jethro, Moses' father-in-law, realised and this is what he wanted to get across to Moses.

There is, first of all *the limit of time*. Exodus 18.13: 'The people stood by Moses from the morning until the evening,' and the task still remained unfinished – it was so vast! It is a simple fact that there is a limit to what one man can do giving all the time he can, and more than he should, to tackling the work he faces. This is true in every department of life. There is a limit to what one man can do, in a given time, in a garden or in a business. There is a limit to what one woman can do in the home; to what one mother can do with a family. This is true also of a Christian worker in a Church. There is a limit that time imposes as to what one person can possibly do; and yet you and I are living in a day when the need is infinitely great. There is so much to do, and seemingly so little time to do it!

Two of my great friends told me recently that at times they had had to do with four hours' sleep, in their work for Christ. One of them has suffered a serious illness; the other has died! Both of them were comparatively young men.

Too much to do and too few to do it: so much to do, and so little time in which to attempt it. So we have to face and reckon with the limit of time in the work of the kingdom of God. Let's face it – there is a limit imposed by time upon what one person can do for the cause of the kingdom.

There is also *the limit of strength*. In Exodus 18.17, we read that Jethro says to Moses, 'The thing that thou doest is not good. Thou wilt surely wear away', or 'wear out', as the A.R.S.V. has it. Again it is a simple fact that there is a physical limit to what one person can do. One of the tragic facts of our modern times is the number of people who are dying in middle age. Not so long ago medical science was claiming that people would live longer. This is sometimes true of those who are old; the old are living to be more elderly, although not always are they living in any adequate sense of the word. Modern drugs can achieve what one doctor has called the 'medicated prolongation of life.'

But while it may be true that many old people are living to be older, the tragic fact is that more people are dying much younger now than ever they did! In an analysis produced in their annual report, one international insurance company pointed out that fifty per cent of deaths of people over forty were due to heart disease! We seem to be living in days when men are overtaxing their reserves of physical strength. This may be due partly to the fact that activities are increasing. Sunday is no longer a day of rest. It is being treated by the majority of people as a day of so-called recreation! It was designed to be a day of physical rest as well as spiritual worship: now it is becoming a day when the body does not rest but is exercised very often to the point of exhaustion!

In addition to the increase in activities there is of course an increase in anxieties. Although we may be living in an age of wonder through the achievements of science, we are living in an age of worry through the allurements of sin. And so people are more burdened today than they ever were. Their strength is being taxed more today than ever it was, and we face the simple fact that there is a limit concerning that which physical strength can achieve. It is important too that in the work of the Christian Church these limits should be sensed. Remember, then, that there is the limit of time and the limit of strength in the work of the kingdom of God. There is only so much that one person can do.

This chapter then goes on to speak of –

THE LOADS THAT SHOULD BE SHARED IN THE WORK OF GOD. In v.18 Jethro says, 'This thing is too heavy for thee; thou art not able to perform it thyself alone.' But what was too much for one pair of shoulders could be carried by many. No doubt many of us have had the experience of attempting to carry a heavy suitcase at an airport or along a railway platform, or maybe a heavy shopping basket along the street, and then we have met someone or someone has come up to us and said, 'That's far too heavy for you to carry alone, let me help you.' What a difference it has made when another hand has grasped the handle of the suitcase, or the handle of the shopping basket! So too in Christian work there are loads that must be shared.

Think of *the size of the task*! Moses was facing an immense task. The people were now safely out of Egypt. In a sense that had been a comparatively simple matter to achieve, for the task did not take too long. But that was not the end of the work that Moses had to do, indeed, it was only the beginning! To look after so many for so long, as he had, for the span of forty years was a gigantic task; far too heavy for one man to carry alone.

So it is with the work of the Church of Jesus Christ. I think very few people pause to consider how massive the task is. Never was it greater than it is today. It includes the seeking of the wayward and the lost; the saving of the despondent and the defeated; and the instruction of the children; the shepherding of the youths; the strengthening of the faith and fellowship of the mature; the visiting of the sick; the comforting of the bereaved; the welcoming of the stranger; the guiding of the bewildered; the arranging of the programmes; the conducting of meetings and services; the preparation and preaching of addresses and lessons; the writing of letters; the shaping of policy; the conducting of weddings; the conducting of funerals; the maintaining of the fabric; the watching over the finance; the caring for the lonely; the praying for the needy; the enriching of the worship; the supporting of the missionaries; and so on. The task is endless: the demands exacting, and yet so much is so often left to so few!

The size of the task is immense. And that is why there must be: *the sharing of the task* (v.21). Jethro says, 'Thou shalt provide able men' (v.22) 'and they shall bear the burden with thee.' Many hands make light work. Trying to carry something alone can be exhausting; trying to carry something with the help of others can be easy. Not that the work of God is ever easy, but it need not sometimes be as exhausting as it is.

There were of course some things that could not be shared. Jethro recognises this (v.19 and 20): 'Be thou for the people to God-ward.' This seems like an anticipation of the words in Acts 6:4: 'We will give ourselves continually to prayer.' There are certain tasks that only certain people can do, but there was much that could be done by others. There was a great deal that could be shared, but it is important to note that those who were to be selected to share in the work were to be 'able men such as feared God' – men of spiritual and moral integrity and quality. This is important, for there is no use attempting Christian work, spiritual work, unless we ourselves are Christian people.

How often the work of the Church is wrecked and ruined by those who are in the work, not for the sake of Christ but for their own sakes – a love of position! They may be gifted in a certain way and simply want an opportunity to exhibit this gift: demanding prominence, seeking power. Such service is more of a hindrance than a help. Christian work needs Christian people, who will go in the name of Christ; who will go for the sake of Christ; who will go in the power of Christ; who will go for the glory of Christ. The load must be shared. If ever there was a day when the Christian members of congregations needed to face up to this it is today.

And so we have considered the limits that should be sensed; the loads that must be shared; we come on now to the last, and indeed most significant point –

THE LIVES THAT COULD BE SAVED IN THE WORK OF GOD. In v.23 Jethro says, 'If thou shalt do this thing thou shalt be able to endure, and all this people shall also go to their place in peace.'

Note two things that Jethro states here. *There is the tragedy that would be avoided*: 'Thou shalt be able to endure.' Oh, the tragedies of lives shortened; of usefulness cut off! The whole history of the Christian Church is studded with the storys of those who have died young, not because they were struck down by some illness that was incurable but because they have been struck down by some illness that was avoidable. This is not something new, but it is becoming more and more of a problem today.

Not so long ago I picked up the biography of Woodbine Willie, the late Rev. G. A. Studdert Kennedy. It was a fascinating book to read because he was a fascinating person. The thing that shocked me was to discover that at the time of his death he was only forty-six years old. The comment was made that he was 'worn out but not worked out.' Worn out!

I wonder how many Christian ministers and missionaries today are dying too young. They are dying because they are worn out; they are not worked out. There is so much that they have still to give to the Church but the load has crushed them. So many are dying so young. One is compelled to ask the question, Is it necessary? In some cases, in the purpose of God, the answer, I am sure, is – yes. Sometimes God needs a life to be lived out at such a pace, and with such devotion, that it makes its own peculiar mark upon the life of the Church. But occasionally one wonders. While it may be necessary sometimes, it doesn't seem to be necessary every time!

The trouble is that so many members of so many congregations are adding to the burden of the work; they are not under it. They make the work harder for their minister, and sometimes these people are not unconverted people, or worldly people, but they are Christians. It may be just that they are lazy; or it may be that they are awkward; or difficult; it may be that they are demanding; it may be either that they are leaving work undone; or doing it badly and so they are adding worry to the whole task. And because of this, because of the fact that they are not under the load there is tragedy, and some minister dies young, some missionary never comes home.

This was the peril in which Jethro saw Moses. If thou shalt do this thing 'thou shalt be able to endure'. The tragedy would be avoided.

But Jethro was also concerned with: *the efficiency that would be achieved.* 'And all this people shall go to their place in peace.' The work that should be done would be done; the need would be met; the hearts would be blessed. In other words, if more people tackle the job, the job would be better done! We all know the saying 'Many hands make light work', but I question if there ever was a time when so

24

few hands were engaged in the work of the Church of Jesus Christ as today.

There are difficulties everywhere: not enough Sunday school teachers; not enough choir members; so few turning up at the prayer meeting; and yet never was the task so great, never was the need so urgent.

And so we end this study by asking the question with which we began it – 'Are you helping with the burdens today or are you adding to them?' Are you helping with the burdens by your prayers? By your loyalty? By your dependability? By your devotion to Christ? by your willingness to do or not to do? By your availability, at any time, for any task? Are you one of those that 'bear the burden'? My friend Alan Redpath once said, 'Every Christian is either a missionary or a mission-field!' Which are you – part of the burden or under the burden?

3

SAMUEL: WHAT CAN HAPPEN IN
OLD AGE?

'And it came to pass, when Samuel was old. . .'

(1 Samuel 8.1).

The discovery of this text and its suggestiveness, I owe to Dr. Raymond Edman, who was, for many years, President of Wheaton College near Chicago. I remember well visiting the College and having the privilege of addressing the student body. As a memento, Dr. Edman gave me two or three of his books and in one of them, called *The Disciplines of Life*, he had a chapter entitled, 'The Discipline of Declining Days', which, I must confess, seemed to me a slightly depressing title. But its title text is our text for this study: 'And it came to pass, when Samuel was old.' I want to change the title and, in some ways, alter the theme. I would like to call our study, 'Sunset Glory'.

Many years ago I heard the late Fred Mitchell say something that shook me: 'Few Christians end well!' We know that advancing years can be rather tragic physically and mentally, but there is no greater tragedy than when advancing years end badly spiritually. But, here, at least, in Samuel, we have one who proved himself an exception to the rule, if rule there be.

We use some lovely words to describe the declining years of life, and one of them is when we speak of life's eventide. The evening is the hour of the sunset. That's why I want us to title our theme 'Sunset Glory'. If it seems to young people as if I am now going to address myself only to the older generation, I don't think that it is out of place that I should do so, because we don't often hear a message that is for those who are getting on in years. Anyway, most of us when we are young have something to do with older folk in our family circles, or where we work. And, ultimately one day, we who are young are going to be old ourselves, whether we like it or not!

What, then, does the Bible have to say about these later years in life? I want us to note, first of all, what I have called –

THE SHADOWS OF THE SUNSET. We must all have seen wonderful sunsets that left us almost speechless. I have seen many in many lands. But, I think, possibly the most magnificent of all was a sunset I saw in Hout Bay in South Africa. I had been taken for a long drive to see the beauties of the mountains which turned out to be shrouded in mist. But when we left the mountains and the mists and the rain and drove down to Hout Bay, we arrived there just as the sun was setting. When we came out of the valley and the bay lay before us, I could hardly believe my eyes. Both sea and the sky and the mountains surrounding the Bay seemed aflame with fire and colour! It was stupendous. For some, it may have been an unforgettable sunset that was seen nearer home on my own beloved West Coast of Scotland, behind the Arran Hills or over Oban Bay, behind the mountains Mull or Morven. For others the sunset may have been seen at some great altitude when flying in an airliner. I remember one such sunset away up above the Sahara Desert as we flew into the night.

But the one thing that I have always noticed is that the beauty is always multiplied when there are clouds and shadows finding a place in the panorama of splendour. When the sun is setting in a clear sky there is very little beauty. When it is setting amid the clouds, then there is splendour and beauty. Yes, there can be shadows amid the glory of the sunset.

When you and I look at the sunset years in the life of Samuel, we find that there were two areas where the shadows were dark. First of all, we can see *the work that seemed to have been forgotten.* In 1 Samuel 8.5 we read that, 'All the elders gathered themselves together and said to Samuel, "Thou art old, make us a king like all the nations."' There can sometimes be something very heartless about the attitude of those who are younger towards those who are older; a heartlessness that smacks even of ingratitude. It is hard to be told bluntly that we are no longer wanted in the place where we have worked so long and done so much. Is there any more difficult word for an older person to accept than the word we hear in my country far too often today – redundant?

Right from the very beginning there had been a special quality about Samuel's work as prophet and judge of Israel; something that men had instinctively recognised, making his work not simply different but outstanding. In 1 Samuel 3.20 we read, 'All Israel knew that Samuel was established to be a prophet of the Lord.' His was a ministry that was to influence thousands; the whole nation knew the impact of this man's life and work. We read in 1 Samuel 4.1, 'The word of Samuel came to all Israel.' And in 1 Samuel 7.15 we read, 'Samuel judged Israel all the days of his life.' But now, with that record behind him, he wasn't wanted. His place was to be filled by somebody else. 'Thou art old, give us a king.' It is never easy to give up a work that we have loved, a work in which we have been blessed and used by God. It is never easy to give way to another, to step aside and to see another step in. It is never easy to find that the very people to whom we have given our life don't want us anymore. This can happen in a home. How many old people's homes are filled with old people whose children just don't want them any more? This can happen in a job! It can happen in a church! This is the shadow of knowing that the work we have done seems to have been forgotten.

But there was another dark shadow in the life of Samuel when we think of *the ways that seemed to have been for-saken.* In 1 Samuel 8.3 we read, 'His sons walked not in his ways, but turned aside.' And in v.5 we read of the cry of the people, 'Make us a king like all the nations.' Both in the home and in the land change was the order of the day. The

28

years of theocracy and the rule of God through His judges were ending and the monarchy was to take its place. How hurtful was the conduct of his own sons who 'walked not in his ways'. Had their new ways been better ways, it wouldn't have mattered. But their new ways were not better. We read that, 'They walked not in his ways, but turned aside after gain and took bribes and perverted judgment.' They had been intended to follow on in their father's footsteps and there is something desperately sad in their failure to do just that.

I wonder sometimes if the only way that the devil can get his own back on a greatly-honoured servant of God is through his home and through his children. If you have been blessed with godly parents, take care. I think of one of the most greatly-used servants of God that I have ever known, and I have known many, and I watched that man go through the agony of seeing his only son in mature life sent to prison! Both the nature of the offence and the passing of the sentence must have broken the old man's heart! Remember, then, that if the devil can't get at your godly parents directly, his other way is to hurt them through you, if you are young!

How hurtful was the attitude of the people. 'Make us a king *like all the nations*.' It is possible to argue that the monarchy was in the plan of God for Israel, but not just at that moment and certainly not with that king! In Deuteronomy 17.14-15 we read, 'When thou art come unto the land and shalt say, I will set a king over me. Thou shalt set a king over thee *whom the Lord thy God shall choose*.' If that was so, then the sin of the people was more in the motive than in the request. Behind their request was the rejection of the authority of God and the desire for conformity with the ungodly nations around them. When Samuel speaks to them warningly of the effects of the reign of the king, 'which **ye** shall have chosen', it may well have been in his mind that there was a king whom God had chosen. That king was too young at that moment to ascend the throne. That king's name was David. But the impatience and insistence of the people landed them with Saul and all the disasters that came with him. At home and in the nation the old ways seemed to have been forsaken. His work forgotten and his ways forsaken. 'Thou art old, make us a king.' These were some of the shadows of the sunset. And let us face it, there are sorrows and sadnesses that belong to the latter years of life which are peculiarly the prerogative of that time. To find, suddenly, that we are unwanted; how hurtful that can be, how darkening the sky!

Then, secondly, I want us to think of –

THE SERENITY OF THE SUNSET. The hour of sunset is very often the hour when the wind drops. There is a stillness among the trees. There is not a leaf rustling. There is a quietness in the air. There is a calming of the waters. It is a time of quietness and stillness.

Sometimes we manage to get up to a little cottage that we rent on the West Coast of Scotland, on the back road between Oban and Connel Ferry. In the evening, at the hour of the setting of the sun, I love to go and stand at the door. So often, there is not a sound to be heard, except, maybe, in the distance, the bleating of a sheep or the call of curlew.

So it was with Samuel! There was going to be so much less to do. Life's pace would slow down. It would have been understandable if the next thing recorded was either his obituary notice or a reaction of bitterness and resentment. That would have been so understandable, although it would have poisoned his latter days. There could well have been resentment seething and surging in his heart. But these are not found, and his obituary notice doesn't appear for another seventeen eventful chapters! There is not a sound of any stormy resentment and bitter acrimony anywhere. Instead, we find this man of God turning quietly to the other work that God had for him to do. More work, but different work. Indeed, as we shall see, bigger work, and better work. What form did it take?

The ministry of intercession. We find this in 1 Samuel 12.23, when he tells the people, 'God forbid that I should sin against the Lord in ceasing to pray for you.' There is, after all, at least one kind of work that no one can ever stop the servant of God from doing, and that is the ministry of prayer and of intercession! Indeed, the verdict of history was one that placed Samuel alongside Moses as a man of prayer. In Psalm Ninety-nine and verse six, we read of Moses and Aaron, 'Among his priests, and Samuel, among them that called upon the Lord, and He answered them.'

What burdens Samuel was to carry in his latter years! Not burdens of administration; the time for that was past, and Samuel had the good sense to accept that fact – not administration, but intercession! To that ministry of prayer Samuel was able to bring all the wealth of his experience and that insight which the passing of the years and the proving of his God had given to him.

Now, if it is true, and surely it is, that 'more things are wrought by prayer than this world dreams of', then the best work, the biggest work of Samuel was now possible. The time and strength that had been given to so much else could now be given to this. He had time, now, that he never had had before. He had more time to do more work. The turbulence and busyness of another kind of work were ended for good. May God give us grace to see when that time comes and to let one kind of work go, so that different work may be taken up! Samuel saw it and gave himself to it, the ministry of intercession and prayer. Surely this is the biggest job that any believer can do. If you are a Christian, when you get into the retirement years you may well have more time to pray than you have ever had before!

But there was another kind of work that Samuel now found himself involved in. Not just the ministry of intercession, but *the ministry of instruction*. He said, 'Not only will I not sin against the Lord in ceasing to pray for you, but *I will teach* you the good and the right way.' This was to be, however, not so much a public ministry, as a very personal, private and individual ministry of instruction, inspiration, encouragement and counsel. So we find that it was to Samuel that David went again and again. David was aware of God's purpose for his life, but he was baffled and bewildered by the circumstances that threatened his very

31

survival. As yet, he had not been anointed king. To whom did he turn? To Samuel, an old man who gave him counsel and encouragement. All that Paul was to Timothy, Samuel was to David. And when David found his way to Ramah, it was to find Samuel surrounded by other young men who, recognising the worth and wealth of Samuel's experience, had gathered there too. Samuel realised that this was a strategic work and was responsible for bringing into being the first of what came to be known as the Schools of the Prophets.

There is, then, a ministry that only age can exercise if it is willing to give it, and if youth is willing to receive it. I remember when I started my Christian service of preaching the Word of God how I listened to some of the veterans of the battle whom it was my privilege to hear and at whose feet it was my privilege to sit, and in whose company it was my privilege to find myself. When I listened to these men and women speaking with all the weight and authority of fifty or sixty years of walking with God behind them, I envied them, for they had something I knew I didn't have.

Dr. Alexander Whyte comments on Samuel's age and his ministry of counsel and encouragement in this way.

It is only the old and the ripe and the much experienced and the men fullest of past service who can do Samuel's service for our generation and the generation which is coming after us. No amount of talent, no amount of loyalty, no amount of humility, even, can make up in the young, whether in young statesmen or young churchmen, for the wisdom and the experience and the standing and the influence of those getting on in years.

It may not be so much a public ministry, but a more personal and private one that will be carried out in the quieter days that advancing years can bring. But the partnership of age and youth is one of the most wonderful things about the service of God. I will never be able to evaluate or thank God enough for the influence that Bishop Taylor Smith had on my life as a young man in my very early twenties. He was seventy. I was almost fifty years younger. But the counsel and the encouragement that he gave me was something that I shall never forget. I have never forgotten the time when he asked me an awkward question, the meaning of which I didn't know. We had been talking about the programme of the meetings I had arranged for him. He suddenly swung around and said, 'Have you sanctified yourself for me?' I just didn't know what he meant. And so I said, 'Sir, I don't know whether I have or not. I have been praying about these meetings. Others have been praying, too. And we have been preparing. We hope they are going to go well in answer to prayer.' The Bishop replied, 'That is not what I meant. Our Lord said, concerning Himself and His relationship to His disciples, "For their sakes I sanctify myself." Our Lord set Himself apart to be a blessing to them. Have you set yourself apart to be a blessing to me?' And I thought, 'Me . . . be a blessing to him?' He went on, 'I expect to be a blessing to you and I expect you to be a blessing to me. To help you to remember this, I will give you a little prayer of five words. Here it is, based upon the Words of our Lord, "For their sakes I sanctify myself, . . . For Thee, for them, Amen."'

I have never forgotten that encounter nor that wonderful prayer. How often it comes almost instinctively to my lips. You could remember it, too, and bring it to the office, into the hospital ward, into the classroom, standing on your doorstep, setting out for work in the morning, just pause for a moment and offer up that prayer: 'For Thee, for them, Amen.'

I think, again, of an old lady, a widow of a minister, who meant so much to me as a young man. She would have been about eighty, I suppose. I think again of another lady, the wife of a professor at that time. What a lot of these older people meant to me as a young man. There is, then, a ministry, not simply of intercession but of instruction, of inspiration, of encouragement, which older people give to younger ones. Samuel turned himself to that.

33

So we have noted the Serenity of the Sunset as well as the Shadows of it. Finally, let us note what I have called –

THE SPLENDOUR OF THE SUNSET. Has it ever struck you that sunset is often the loveliest time of the day? The Bible speaks in very similar language about old age. In Proverbs 16.31, it tells of the hoary head, the grey head, that is, 'a crown of glory, if it be found in the way of the righteousness'. What made up the splendour of the sunset years in Samuel's life? Two very wonderful things; first we have *the intimacy of his walk with God*. Twice reference is made in very similar terms. In 1 Samuel 8.21 we read, 'Samuel heard all the words of the people and he rehearsed them *in the ears* of the Lord.' In 1 Samuel 9.15, 'Now the Lord had told Samuel *in his ear* a day before Saul came.' Samuel and the Lord seemed to be so close to each other that each had, as we would say, the other's ear. The older Samuel got, the closer he got, until in a wonderful way he was as close to God as it was possible for a man to be. It would seem as if the one just needed to whisper to the other and he heard. The Intimacy of His Walk With God!

The other thing that made up the splendour of the sunset years was *the quality of his work for God*. It's significant to me that the biggest job Samuel ever did, he did when he was old. And what job was that? Surely it was when he found David. I often stand back and look in wonder that it was an old retired servant of God whom God used to summon David to be king. It was my privilege to know the late Mr. Lindsay Glegg for many, many years. I remember so clearly hearing him in my young days, but Lindsay Glegg never retired. Oh, he retired from business, but possibly the biggest thing he ever did for God was something he did when he had passed his seventieth birthday. That was when God gave him the vision of starting as a follow-up to the Billy Graham Crusade at Harringay, London, a Christian holiday crusade at a Butlin Camp at Filey, where the attendances beginning at a figure of fifteen hundred, have risen every year until now, twenty-five years later, more than six thousand come year after year.

It may well be true that few of God's servants end well, but could anyone have ended better than Samuel? When at last the news broke on a stunned nation that Samuel had died, we read in 1 Samuel 25.1, that 'All the Israelites were gathered together and lamented him'.

We have thought of the shadows of the sunset and the work that seemed to have been forgotten and the ways that seemed to have been forsaken. We have thought of the serenity of the sunset, the ministry of intercession, the ministry of instruction. We have thought of the splendour of the sunset, the intimacy of his walk with God, and the quality of his work for God. Dr. Edman called it the 'Discipline of Declining Days'. That has a slightly negative sound about it to me, but when I came to analyse this wonderful story of a life, of the things that can happen when a man is old, I felt that the only words to describe it were the two words, 'Sunset Glory'. I want, however, to end with a poem that Dr. Edman quotes. It seems to sum it up. It seems to express the longing to end well.

I want the faith that envies not
The passing of the days;
That sees all times and ways
More endless than the stars;
That looks at life not as a little day
Of heat and strife,
But one eternal revel of delight,
With God, the friend, adventurer, and light.

What matter if one chapter nears the end
What matter if the silver deck the brow
Chanting I go, past crimson, flaming from the autumn hills
Past winter snow.

To find that glad new chapter where God's spring
Shall lift its everlasting voice to sing;
This is the faith I seek
It shall be mine
A faith looks beyond the peaks of time.

(Ralph S. Cushman)

So, for all of us, the sunset hour must come. Let us all remember, however, that the sunset is but the prelude to the dawn!

4

SAMUEL: THE SIN OF PRAYERLESSNESS

'God forbid that I should sin against the Lord in ceasing to pray for you' (1 Samuel 12.23).

From time to time it is a good and indeed a wise thing that as Christians we should concern ourselves with possible areas of failure in our Christian living. There need be nothing unhealthy about this, but simply an attempt at honesty, and a realisation that we should take seriously what it means when the Bible says that 'judgment must begin at the house of God'.

In this connection it is important to realise that sin can be one of two kinds. Sin can consist either in doing what I know to be wrong: 'Sin is the transgression of the law' (1 John 3.4), or sin can consist in the failure to do what I know to be right: 'To him that knoweth to do good and doeth it not to him it is sin' (James 4.17). We call these, theologically, sins of commission and sins of omission. Both are sins, and it is open to question which is the more serious in the eyes of God.

I want us to examine certain aspects of one of the most common sins of omission, though possibly the least felt sin in Christian living, the sin of prayerlessness. It is named to be a sin here in the words of our text, in the words spoken by Samuel. 'God forbid that I should **sin** against the Lord in ceasing to pray for you.' The failure is one that may so easily be charged against any Christian, for prayer is an obligation laid upon every Christian. Luke 18.1 records that Jesus 'spake a parable unto them to this end that men **ought** to pray'. We cannot all preach, but we can all pray. We cannot all give large sums of money, though many of us could give much more than we do, but we can all pray. We cannot all go to the mission-field, we cannot all witness in the open-air, we cannot all lead a meeting for Bible study, but we can all pray. We can all pray in the privacy of our own rooms, we can all pray in the corporate acts of prayer in the worship of our churches. This we can all do. This we all ought to do. Indeed we are promised the help of the Holy Spirit in this very activity in Romans 8.26, and how much we all need help in this area of our Christian life.

But why should prayerlessness be regarded as a sin in the life of the Christian? Is this an area in which the old saying is relevant that 'familiarity breeds contempt'? Are we as Christians so familiar with a state of prayerlessness that we have ceased to feel there is anything wrong about it, indeed to recognise that it is sinful?

I want to suggest that prayerlessness in the life of a Christian is sin in the first place because by prayerlessness –

THE CROSS OF CHRIST IS DESPISED. This is the case because right at the heart of the Christian experience is the fact that one of the privileges of being a Christian is that we have the right of access to God, and that privilege is one which we are meant to enjoy and exercise, one moreover, that has been dearly bought.

The Christian Church has been divided and has argued as to which symbol is the true symbol of the Christian faith, a cross or a crucifix. Without going into the answer to that question which might be controversial, I would like to suggest that the first symbol of the heart of the Christian faith was neither! The first symbol, wrought not out of the thoughts of men, but out of the mind of God, was the rent veil of the Temple, rent from the top to the bottom, and therefore rent by the hand of God. The message was loud and clear, that sinners could now, through the work of Christ, find their way into the presence of a Holy and righteous God, that the way into a new relationship of fellowship was now wide open for all to enter, if they so chose to do.

In this connection I want us to note two things, and the first is *the untold price* of this access, a price which John describes in his first epistle, in 1 John 2.1-2, as the making of a propitiation, or, to be more precise, Christ as being in Himself 'the propitiation for our sins, and not for ours only, but also for the sins of the whole world'. John is here confirming the prophetic words of John the Baptist when he first saw Christ and cried out, 'Behold the Lamb of God which taketh away the sin of the world'. Paul refers to this price when writing to Timothy in 1 Timothy 2.4-5 he writes how God 'will have all men to be saved' and how, to make that possible, 'Christ . . . gave Himself a ransom for all'. And let there be no theological devaluation of the blood of Christ and let not the price, the infinite worth of the Son of God, be cut down to suit some theological theory worked out in the minds of men and not declared in the Word of God.

The veil of the temple, be it noted, was rent in twain only when 'Jesus had cried with a loud voice, "it is finished",' when the price was paid! It is this new relationship, thus made possible for sinful men at such infinite cost, which includes the privilege of prayer.

This is what the writer of the letter to the Hebrews has in mind when he says that we are to have 'boldness to enter into the holiest by the blood of Jesus, by a new and living way, which He hath consecrated for us, through the veil, that is to say His flesh. Let us draw nigh . . .' (Hebrews 10.19-20). This too is surely what Paul had in mind when he wrote, 'Being justified by faith, we have peace with God through our Lord Jesus Christ, by Whom we have access . . .' (Romans 5.1-2). The untold price was a price paid not by man, but by God, it was a price beyond all human calculation and paid so that we might have the right to come into His very presence and indeed live in that presence.

But when I think of the sin of prayerlessness, I think not only of the untold price, but of *the untrod path*. The price has been paid, that path has been opened, but the path is so seldom used. How hurtful this must be to the heart of God; what despite we do to the Cross of Christ when we fail to

39

take advantage of the privilege it has bestowed upon us.

Prayer is spoken of by Christ as being one of the normalities of the Christian life. Recall His words in Matthew 6, '**When** thou prayest. . .' He does not say, '**If** thou prayest. . .' Christ assumes that His people will pray, and that first of all behind a closed door in secret. His teaching extended to include a praying together with others: 'If two of you shall agree on earth as touching anything ye shall ask, it shall be done for them of my Father which is in heaven.' The early Church practised this togetherness in prayer from Pentecost onwards. This access into the very presence of God was made possible so that it would be used. The privilege is meant to be valued. The gift is meant to be treasured. The untrod path does despite to the untold price. Everytime we neglect the path, we despise the Cross which opened it.

Is it any wonder, then, that we speak of the sin of prayerlessness, when it means that we treat the Cross thus? Have you ever thought of it like that? Or have you thought of prayerlessness simply as a kind of slackness, a kind of spiritual laziness that does not really matter very much? I suggest to you that we need to rethink our thinking in this area. Prayerlessness is sin because by it the Cross of Christ is despised, and despised by those of us who name ourselves Christians.

The second thing that comes to mind when we ponder this crucial matter is that because of prayerlessness –

THE CHURCH OF CHRIST IS DEPRIVED. I gather this from the fact that not only is there an access that the Christian is meant to enjoy in prayer, but that there are answers which the Christian is meant to receive in prayer. Nothing is clearer, from both Scripture and history, than that prayer does something, or if you prefer it, that prayer enables God to do something that otherwise He would not do. We sing in one of our hymns that

> Prayer moves the arm that moves the world
> To bring salvation down.

Or if we are among those who have enjoyed singing some of the lovely choruses that I myself was taught to sing in my younger days, we may well have sung the words 'Prayer changes things'. If the hymn-writer and the chorus-writer are right, then presumably the absence of prayer means that things are not changed, and that the arm that moves the world does not move. We however do not need these kinds of witness, when we have the word of God to tell us in James 4.2, 'Ye have not because ye ask not.'

Let us then take note of *the encouragement to prayerfulness* we find in the Word of God. We find these encouragements not only in the Word of God which is, of course, our ultimate and final authority, but also in experience. We face an obvious statement when we say that the Bible is full of promises which assure us that our God is one that both hears and answers prayer. We must not, of course, overlook the fact that conditions are imposed as well. There is nothing unconditional about prayer. The psalmist warns us that 'If I regard iniquity in my heart, the Lord will not hear me', indicating that the unrepentant sinner, the rebel, will not be heard. James tells us, 'Ye ask and receive not, because ye ask amiss'. The prayer that is purely and utterly selfish is quite unacceptable to God. Prayers that are not 'in the name of Jesus', that is to say, not in harmony with the character of Christ, will find no response either.

But granting all that, and much more besides – recognising that God's answer may be 'yes'; it may be 'no'; it could be 'wait'; or that God's answer could be what we need rather than what we want – we still face the fact that the witness of the promises found in the Word of God encourage us to pray, and to pray confidently. Jesus Himself said, 'Ask and ye shall have, seek and ye shall find, knock and it shall be opened unto you. For everyone that asketh receiveth, and he that seeketh findeth, and to him that knocketh, it shall be opened.' The God of the Bible is a God who both hears and answers prayer. And still we fail to pray!

But if there are these encouragements to prayer, surely this means, equally, that there can and indeed must be *an*

41

impoverishment through prayerlessness; 'Ye have not because ye ask not,' says James. I feel that there is something that every Christian and every Church needs to face. The resources are there in the grace of God to meet our needs, but they have never been tapped. Try to catch the vision for a moment! God has placed every Christian at the centre of expanding circles of contact, contact with human need that can only be met through the grace of God, need of which a Christian may well be the only person who has the knowledge. The need may be within the circle of home and family, among our neighbours, within the circle of our church, our colleagues where we work. I quoted the words of James, 'Ye have not because ye ask not'. Maybe we could equally truly say, 'They have not because we ask not'. Oh, the impoverishment through prayerlessness! Is it any wonder that the Bible speaks of prayerlessness as sin, not only because the Cross of Christ is despised, not only because the Church of Christ is deprived, but also for another very significant reason.

Prayerlessness is sin in the Bible because through it –

THE CAUSE OF CHRIST IS DEFEATED. I say this because I find in the Christian life as set out in the Word of God not only that there is this access that we are meant to enjoy, not only are there these answers that we are meant to receive, but there are also attacks that we are meant to repel.

'Upon this rock I will build my church,' said Jesus Christ, 'and the gates of hell shall not prevail against it.' Right through the New Testament we find the language of battle and of conflict. In Ephesians 6.12-18 Paul reminds the Christians at Ephesus of the spiritual conflict upon which they will be engaged. His description of the Christian's armour ends with a reference to what John Bunyan in *Pilgrim's Progress* calls 'the weapon of all-prayer'. 'Praying always with all prayer and supplication in the spirit, watching thereunto with all perseverance and supplication for all saints.' This passage recalls another in 2 Corinthians 10.3-4, where Paul writes, 'Ye do not war after the flesh, for the weapons of our warfare are not carnal but mighty through God.' What searching truths these are that we have been thinking over, how the Cross of Christ can be despised, how the Church of Christ can be deprived, and now finally how the Cause of Christ can be defeated.

Think for a moment of *the warfare in which we are engaged*. Let us never forget that we are up against spiritual forces of evil. 'We wrestle not against flesh and blood, but against principalities, against powers, against the rulers of the darkness of this world, against spiritual wickedness in high places.' If the language of our Authorised Version sounds a little bit unreal, does this translation help you? 'Our fight is not against any physical enemy; it is against organisations and powers that are spiritual, we are up against the unseen, the power that controls this dark world, and spiritual agents from the very headquarters of evil.'

We are in a battle, and it is a battle against spiritual forces against which human weapons are powerless and futile. But if there is a war in which we are engaged, there are also *the weapons with which we are equipped* – and among these is the weapon of prayer. To go into battle without our weapons, or even without one vital one of them, is to go out into defeat. Indeed it is to be defeated almost before the battle has even commenced!

When you and I talk about defeat we so often think in terms that are personal, but what about the defeat that is corporate. Is your church a defeated Church? Wherever the Church lives victoriously it lives prayerfully. When revival swept the church of Robert Murray McCheyne in Dundee, he tells us that thirty-nine prayer meetings were going on every week, and that five of them were attended entirely by children! Surely here we can lay our finger upon what may be the cause of the failure of so many churches to make even the shadow of an impact upon the world around. How many prayer meetings are attended by members of your church? How many people are found at prayer meetings out of the total membership of your congregation? Maybe you cannot go every week, you have other responsibilities, but do you never go? Maybe with a bit of planning you could go. You see, there is an attack we are meant to be able to repel. You and I are meant to win. The Church is meant to advance.

When Christ was raised from the dead on that first Easter morning it was a moment of triumph. It spelt out victory. Yet that note of victory and of triumph, that sense of advance and of achievement, that sense of power and progress, all these have almost died right out of the experience not only of the average Christian but also of the average church, and out of our thinking, let alone our experience. I picked up a book the other day written by Lilias Trotter of North Africa, and one little sentence stood out with a note of challenge to me. She said, 'Fighting does not mean standing up and being hit!' Somehow or other I feel that is just about all that too many of us know. We are just standing up as Christians and are being hit. People are hitting us; we are not making any advance, any impact upon our world. There is no sense of advance or of achievement. We are just being knocked about by everyone and everything.

But that is not what God ever intended! True, we will be hit, there will be wounds in the battle, there always are. There are sometimes casualties, and they are usually treated with kindness in ordinary warfare. Alas, in spiritual warfare casualties are so often treated with contempt. Let's face it, there will be wounds, there will be casualties, but with both of these God's intention is that there should be victory as well, there should be progress, there should be advance, the enemy ought to be defeated.

Is it possible that the reason is that the Church has forgotten, the average Christian has forgotten to use the most powerful piece of equipment that God has provided? Let us then face the fact that prayerlessness in the Bible is sin. We have found the reason it is thus named in the Word of God: the Cross is Despised, the Church is Deprived and the Cause is Defeated! Somebody once said, and I have never forgotten the sentence, that 'The worst sins of the Christian Church are not those that the world sees to be sins.' The world does not see anything wrong about a man who never spends a minute in prayer from the moment he wakes up to the moment he goes to bed at night. The world does not think ill of such a man, but what does God think of a Christian who lives like that? There was a time when, in some circles of the Christian Church if a lady had added a touch of paint to colour her lips, eyebrows would be raised and criticism would be offered. But so often those who might comment about the lady who had paint *on* her lips, would be Christians who had no prayer *on* their own lips. I do not think God would be as concerned about the presence of paint on the one pair of lips, as He would be about the absence of prayer from the other pair of lips!

Possibly some of the greatest sinners in the sight of God are not the men who on a Saturday night come reeling out of a pub the worse for drink, but some very respectable Christians making their way home not guilty of the sin of drunkenness, but of the sin of prayerlessness, for let us all remember that, as far as the Bible goes, prayerlessness is sin.

5

NATHAN: THE CORONATION OF THE KING

'Who shall sit on the throne?' (1 Kings 1.20)

I remember many years ago hearing Dr. S. D. Gordon, a visitor from America, saying something which has remained in my mind. He said, 'In every heart there is a throne and a cross. If Jesus is on the throne, self is on the cross. If self is on the throne, Jesus is on the cross.' I wonder if some of us have found ourselves in the position where we realise rather uncomfortably, vividly, that the issue for us, and in our lives, centres around just that very thing? Is Jesus Christ going to occupy the throne? As a guide to our thoughts and a direction to our meditation I want to turn with you to a familiar story from 1 Kings 1.20. There we find this question. Bathsheba is speaking, and she says, 'And thou, my lord, O king, the eyes of all Israel are upon thee, that thou shouldest tell them who shall sit on the throne of my lord the king after him.'

'Who shall sit on the throne?' The story that moves around this question begins at v.5, and there are three ingredients that make up the complete pattern. And in v.5 the story of this crisis in the life of David the king begins with the discovery of –

THE RIVAL TO A THRONE. 'Then Adonijah the son of Haggith exalted himself, saying, I will be king: and he prepared him chariots and horsemen, and fifty men to run before him. And his father had not displeased him at any time in saying, Why has thou done so? and he was also a very goodly man; and his mother bare him after Absalom.'

A rival to a throne: for we have to take that statement of

Adonijah, who exalted himself saying 'I will be king,' and put it against the background of the purpose of God. The purpose of God had been revealed to David many years before, and it was this, that the throne of David was designed for Solomon. In 1 Chronicles 22.8 we read, 'But the word of the Lord came to me, saying, Thou hast shed blood abundantly, and hast made great wars . . . thou shalt not build an house unto my name . . . Behold, a son shall be born to thee, who shall be a man of rest . . . He shall build an house for my name; and he shall be my son, and I shall be his father; and I will establish the throne of his kingdom over Israel for ever.' The purpose of God, which is the background of this story, was that the throne of David was reserved for Solomon; and I want to suggest to you that one greater than Solomon is here, and that throne in your life and mine is designed for one greater than Solomon.

Is there a rival to the throne in your life? There was in David's. 'Adonijah exalted himself saying, I will be king.' What about this rival, what about this Adonijah? The first thing that we read about him concerns *the indulgence that David had always showed.* Verse 6: 'And his father had not displeased him at any time in saying, Why has thou done so? and he also was a very goodly man.' Here was a spoilt son, an indulged son. Here was an affection that was undisciplined. Here was someone in David's life to whom David was unable to say 'No'. I wonder whether there is a similar indulgence in your life? I wonder whether there is something in your life to which you never say 'No'?

'He was a goodly man.' I wonder whether that means he was attractive? I wonder whether that suggests that he was a handsome, delightful person? I wonder whether this indulgence of yours is arrayed in attraction and held in deep affection, and you can never say 'No'. Is it the world with all its allurements? Is it some particular realm of your life where you just can never say 'No', that's all? That is what Adonijah was – one to whom David had always shown indulgence, one to whom David could never say 'No'.

But the extraordinary thing is – and how true this is to life – that the one to whom this indulgence had always been shown was one in whose heart there was *an intention that David had never sensed*. David never dreamt for one moment that Adonijah was determined to get the throne; an intention that David had never sensed, and yet, there it was. Adonijah, the son, exalted himself, saying, 'I will be king'. I wonder whether you ever sense the intention that the enemy of your souls has nurtured and nourished for so long? This weakness that in your life is the focus of his activity, of his purpose; and there it is, attractive, indulged, held in affection, but you do not know what underlies that smiling face. Do you know what does? An intention is aimed at the throne which God has set apart for one greater than Solomon. It is the throne that he wants. Have you realised that there is only One who has the right to your throne? And that leads me on to the second aspect of this theme and incident and crisis in the life of David. It begins with the uncovering of a rival to a throne, and then it goes on to speak of –

THE REPROACH ON A NAME. That is implied, is it not, in the words of Bathsheba in v.20: 'And thou, my lord, O king, the eyes of all Israel are upon thee, that thou shouldest tell them who shall sit on the throne of my lord the king.' David had a name, a name that was greatly beloved; and you and I have a name, a name that is even more beloved, for the name of Christ is woven into our name. I wonder whether in your life there is present what was present in the life of David – a wonderment that centred round him. People were puzzled as they watched him. 'The eyes of all Israel are upon thee, that thou shouldest tell them who shall sit on the throne.' Everybody knew of the purpose of God, everybody knew that Solomon was destined to be king, everybody knew that the throne was meant to be his: yet here was Adonijah. *A wonder that centred round him*; and everywhere in the land David's name was the talking point, and every time they talked about him they wondered, and said, 'What is David doing?'

Is your name a talking point among other Christians,

among the world? Are many eyes upon you – far more than you think – seeing more than you think, knowing more than you give them credit for? They all know that the name of Christian involves the throne handed to Him, and they are baffled and puzzled, and there is wonderment in other people's minds, and they say, 'What has happened to David?' And some people say that about you; they say, 'What has happened?' the other nurses in the hospital, the other friends in the office, the other members of the church, the other members of the presbytery.

Is there a wonderment that centres round you? Is your name a talking point because people are baffled by this extraordinary contradiction that they can see, that the purpose of God is not being fulfilled in your life? They can see that which is dominating your life, and it is not the will of God. It is alien to the Spirit of God, and your name is a talking point.

And then, *the witness that was borne to him*. It came through Nathan the prophet of God, who first of all approached Bathsheba, and then Bathsheba conveyed the message to the king. This man had such a wonderful name, and yet now there was a reproach on the name. What was it? It was a very faithful witness, the word of a friend; and the word was this – v.11 and v.17, to take the actual words spoken to David, 'My lord, thou sweareth by the Lord thy God unto thine handmaid, saying, Assuredly Solomon thy son shall reign after me, and he shall sit upon my throne. And now, behold, Adonijah reigneth; and now, my lord the king, thou knowest it not.' The word that came to him was the word of truth, and oh, how faithful his friends were, Nathan and Bathsheba, 'Adonijah doth reign, and David our lord knoweth it not' (v.11). Do you know, one of the most tragic breakdowns in Christian fellowship is the breakdown of friendship which fails to tell the truth. And one of the appalling tragedies of Christian living is that Christians can become a talking point in their circle because of a breakdown in their relationship with Jesus Christ, and everybody talks about it to one another, but never to them.

I wonder whether you have found a more faithful Friend than any human friend? Have you? 'Faithful are the wounds of a friend.' Has 'the Friend that sticketh closer than a brother' spoken to you? Has some prophet of God, has the very Spirit of God, come and said to you, 'The throne designed for a greater than Solomon is occupied already.' 'Adonijah doth reign.' You did not know it, but people have been talking about it for weeks, for months, for years – and not one of your friends has told you. Has that Friend come and told you something? Something that has hurt, something that has come right in and touched this that you love, even as David loved his son? But there has not only been the rival to the throne in your life; there has been the reproach on a name, and your Christian witness and testimony at the moment is a shadowed, clouded thing. Is it? For this story ends, I think, wonderfully. Beginning with the rival to a throne, continuing with the unveiling of the reproach on a name, and ending with –

THE RESOLVE OF A KING. What was the resolve that David made – and surely here the greatness of David is brought out most vividly and most clearly – what was the resolve of a king in this crisis? It was a twofold resolve. First of all, the resolve that David made meant *the abdication of a throne*. Read on to v.29, for the king is now answering Bathsheba: 'And the king sware, and said, 'As the Lord liveth, that have redeemed my soul out of all distress, even as I sware unto thee by the Lord God of Israel, saying, Assuredly Solomon thy son shall reign after me, and he shall sit upon my throne *in my stead*: even so will I certainly do this day.' That was the abdication of his throne.

Are you ready to abdicate? Are you? There was no delay about this: that revealed the greatness of David. Have you been delaying? Have you been having a controversy with God about this very thing, and you have said, 'Well, I am going to think about it a bit more: I am so fond of Adonijah, he is such a lovely fellow. I am so fond of this thing, I cannot say "no".' It may come from the angle of the world, it may come from the angle of the flesh, it may come from the angle of the devil, but it is focused up into one thing – nine times out of ten into one thing – that has been rivalling the claims of the one greater than Solomon: and God is asking you to do something, not tomorrow, but this day: 'Assuredly Solomon shall reign, and he shall sit upon my throne and in my stead; even so will I certainly do *this day*.' The resolve of a king was the abdication of a throne, in which there was no delay.

Then just one last and, I think, a lovely touch. The resolve of the king meant not only the abdication of a throne in which there was no delay, but it meant *the acclamation of a son*, about which there was no doubt. And we have one greater than Solomon, a greater Son. And David said, 'Call me Zadok the priest, and Nathan the prophet, and Benaiah the son of Jehoida. And they came before the king. The king also said unto them, Take with you the servants of your lord, and cause Solomon my son to ride upon mine own mule, and bring him down to Gihon: and let Zadok the priest and Nathan the prophet anoint him there king over Israel: and blow ye with the trumpet, and say, God save king Solomon. And Zadok the priest took an horn of oil out of the tabernacle, and anointed Solomon. And they blew the trumpet; and all the people said, God save king Solomon' (vv.32-39). And the report reached Adonijah: 'Verily our lord king David hath made Solomon king.' Well, have you done what David did with a greater than Solomon. And it was done with acclamation, with the sound of the trumpet, with the most public action that David could arrange. He said, 'I want every single person in the land to know that Solomon is king.'

A rival, a reproach, a resolve. Who shall sit on the throne? Dr. Paul Rees came to preach in my church in London. Speaking from the well-known text, 'Behold, I stand at the door and knock.' he quoted another preacher as saying that Jesus is only seated when He is on a throne, then he added, 'Where Jesus does not reign, He cannot rest.'

Who shall sit on the throne? The rival? Have you recognised the rival? The reproach: have you faced up to that?

The resolve: have you made it? It meant abdication, and acclamation. And the report spread throughout the land, 'David hath made Solomon king.' And a greater than Solomon is here. Have you made Him King? If you have not, would you like to?

I am going to end with a simple story about the late Queen Mary. I had the privilege of visiting someone who was a close friend of the Royal Family, and she said that when King George VI died and the young Queen Elizabeth came to the throne, so young to accept such a heavy task, Queen Mary, the old Queen Mother, that regal, splendid figure whom many of us knew so well by sight, wrote a letter to her grand-daughter, the new Queen Elizabeth. Do you know how she signed it? 'Your loving Grandmother and devoted Subject.' She had been a Queen herself, but she was now subject to this Queen.

Would you like to sign yourself today, 'Christ's devoted subject,' crying, 'Take the crown and place it upon His brow,' and abdicate in His favour? Will you do it and do it in your own heart, so quietly, so sincerely, that He will be King from today. And then people will say, 'She . . . he . . . has made a greater than Solomon King.' Will you do it, and do it this day? Do it now.

6

THE OLD PROPHET: A PERIL OF SPIRITUAL MATURITY

'Now there dwelt an old prophet in Bethel . . .'
(1 Kings 13.11).

I want to consider with you some aspects of failure in Christian living which are peculiarly the peril of those who have grown older in Christian experience, and do so against the background of this story. And if we want a text to focus our thought at the beginning, we shall take it from 1 Kings 13.11, 'Now there dwelt an old prophet in Bethel . . .'

May I begin by saying that I know perfectly well that *age has its prerogatives*. There are some things that age has that youth can never have. I think, for instance, of the *wealth of experience* that age alone can enjoy. Most of us know what it is to meet older Christians who are rich in experience, who have a wealth of memory, veterans of many battle-fields and conquests; men and women who have walked a long way with God. They have a maturity of judgment, a knowledge of life and of the Bible, a knowledge of God, that seem to make the problems which baffle and perplex us quite simple, and which enable them to avoid the mistakes that those of us who are younger so easily make!

In this wealth of experience they have a prerogative over youth; and also, I believe, in *the work of encouragement*. Many of us can recall meeting Christians the wealth of whose experience has humbled us, and yet these same men and women have accomplished a work of encouragement which has helped us along. But while age and experience have their prerogatives, they also have their *perils*: and it is to these that I want to turn your thoughts.

Let us turn then, and look into the mirror of God's Word. Let us look at this old prophet, and, as we read, I want to remind you that age is a relative term and that through this story God's Word may come to those who are not so very old, but **older**, who dwell 'in Bethel'. And first, I want to note with you what I call –

THE LETHARGY THAT MARKED HIS SERVICE. Here was a man who had spiritually come very nearly to a standstill. Note *the inaction into which he had settled down*. Bethel, where he lived, was the scene of Jeroboam's sin, the setting up of a false religion, served by false priests. The details are found in the closing verses of the previous chapter. The action of the king was to become proverbial and legendary in the history of Israel: for Jeroboam was known as the king 'who made Israel to sin'.

The motive of Jeroboam's sin was no doubt political expediency; the action, one of spiritual apostasy! And in the face of this challenge, the old prophet was silent. He had nothing to say, and said nothing. Why was this? Why had this lethargy settled down across his service for God? Was it because of *weariness*? He had fought through many battles in the past; he just could not rouse himself for yet another battle. This time he would leave it to others to fight. Or perhaps it was *worldly wisdom*, for he had a family to look after, and it would not do to incur disfavour in high places. Would it matter if he compromised just this once, and let this thing pass unrebuked?

Whatever the reasons, the silence remained unbroken, the message unspoken, and the servant of God remained at home. The lethargy that marked his service.

I want to ask, is this, perchance, true of some of us? Is our pace slowing down? Spiritually, vitally, have we very nearly come to a halt and a standstill? There was a time when no one was keener than we were in the ministry of prayer. In our own prayer-life we prayed with some purpose. In the prayer-life of our church we could always be relied upon: our prayers meant so much to the church, to God, to the minister, to ourselves! But in our praying we have slowed down; and for weeks, for months, it may be for years, 'the old prophet' has come almost to a halt in his prayer-life.

In our consecration we were once fastidiously careful; our standards were high, almost intolerably so, in our separation to Christ from the world – but it cost so much to maintain that standard, and we grew so weary, and so wise, that slowly and almost imperceptibly the world encroached, and as far as consecration is concerned, we have almost forgotten the meaning of the word!

What about our service? How desperately keen we were; how unashamedly we used to go out for the conversion of others, and we saw them converted. But that has all stopped now; we are not interested in that; we do not toil for that; we do not preach for that; we do not suffer for that as once we did.

We are Christians still, we are prophets still; we still hold office: we are deacons, we are elders; we are Sunday-School teachers, we are members of committees, chairmen of committees, we are ministers, we are bishops, missionaries, Christian parents, we are holding office! Listen, has all of the spiritual vitality been drained out of our lives and is there a lethargy upon our service and have we come to a halt, are we at a standstill? Our testimony? We have none! Our usefulness has practically gone. We are holding on to positions; we have ranks to which we have ceased to have the spiritual right! The inaction into which he had settled.

And then I want you to notice *the intrusion by which he was startled*. The lethargy which was upon the life of this old prophet was suddenly, rudely startled; the silence which he had been careful to maintain was suddenly, sharply broken. His sons rushed in to tell him of the dramatic event: that the king himself had been officiating at the high place that very day, and then a man of God, a young man of Judah, had dramatically interrupted the service. The curse of God had been pronounced against the altar; and the king, violently angry, had caused the instant arrest of the man of God – only to be struck immediately by the hand of God in judgment! Then a cowed and frightened king had

55

pleaded for mercy, before a rent altar amidst the smoke of the scattered ashes.

A cringing and conciliatory monarch had then offered hospitality and rewards, to find his offer treated with contempt. What had been the words of the man of God from Judah, to the king? 'If thou wilt give me half thine house, I will not go in with thee, neither will I eat bread nor drink water in this place: for so was it charged me by the word of the Lord.' The long silence had been broken, and like a sudden peal of thunder out of a leaden and sullen sky, the voice of God had spoken; and with glowing faces the sons of the old prophet ended their breathless story, while the old man watched and listened!

What was it that turned their glowing faces into puzzled wonderment? Was it the sudden, stabbing realisation that what had just happened should have happened long ago – and that the man who should have done it was not the man of God from Judah, but the old prophet, their father, to whom they now told their story, across whose face consternation and anger now chased each other, until finally a burning, sullen anger settled there? And the man who had been inactive so long was at last stung into action, demanding 'Where did that man of God go?'

The intrusion by which he was startled! All I know is this, that again and again, where the lethargy of our service has slowed down to inaction, when an intrusion comes to startle us into amazement and into anger – when a minister comes to the church with a flaming heart; a son or a daughter is converted in their Christian home to God, and with passionate devotion they give their all to Christ; when a man or a girl joins the fellowship of the Church with heart afire for God; a Christian comes into the office, a new nurse starts her training in the hospital, a new curate joins the staff – and the silence is broken, the lethargy is startled into alarm. God begins to speak directly where there had been a comfortable security and quietness. All is disturbed and confused. And the 'old prophet' amazed, alarmed, angry, is stirred to action at last.

The lethargy that marked his service. . . Is there an old

prophet reading this? Spiritually you have come to a halt. Has somebody come into your life? Has the voice of God spoken.

Worse followed, for the lethargy that marked the service of the old prophet was replaced by what I call –

THE ANIMOSITY THAT SEARED HIS SPIRIT. Here we face the tragic fact that the man who took no action at all against the deeds of Jeroboam became passionately and angrily active against the man of God. One of the things that appals me, that shames me, is just this very thing: The ceaseless animosity of Christian against Christian! You find it in churches, you find it in fellowships, you find it on mission-stations, you find it in societies, you find it wherever you find Christians: and the tragedy is that those involved are very, very seldom youngsters in the faith. Children do not normally kill children. Men kill men. You do not find it in the Sunday School, you do not find it among the young people in the Youth Fellowship, you do not find it among the confirmation candidates. You find it at a higher level. You find it among the older Christians, in your deacons' court, among your elders, in your kirk session; you find it among your clergy and ministers, in your committees, among your Sunday School teachers, in Christian parents; you find it in the 'old prophet'. This is where you find it; the animosity that sears the spirit.

You find to your amazement that those who have ceased to be active in the vital things of God against the enemy of souls are tirelessly active against the 'men of God'. Why? Why was this old prophet roused to action but not against the false worship of Jeroboam: he did not do a thing about that! Why was he roused to action against the faithful servant of Jehovah?

I think, first of all, because of *a pride that would not be humbled*. The man's pride was hurt to the quick. The man who remained unmoved when God's Name was dishonoured was stung to the quick when his own actions were condemned.

Think how the security and comfort he had gained by

compromising his loyalty had been treated with contempt by another. The standards that he had lowered by his slackness had been raised again to the mast by the zealousness of the man of God. The silence he had so carefully maintained had been broken. The message he had ceased to declare had been declared by another. Everything he knew he should have been, and had failed to be, the man of God from Judah had been.

As his own sons told the story of it all, they told the story of his own condemnation; and his pride hated it. A man in his position, a man of his age, a man of his experience, being condemned, being judged! He had been weighed in the balances, and found wanting. Not explicitly, for the man of God from Judah had not said a word about him: but he had been condemned implicitly. He sensed it as he listened to the story told by his own sons. He saw it in the glow that had been kindled, and still shone on their faces. His imagination ran riot as he followed the telling of the story in a thousand homes in Bethel that day; and with the telling he would have been called 'the old prophet, the man who had done nothing, the man who had lowered his standards, the man who had compromised. . .' Condemned! Condemned . . . and *he hated it*.

Have you got a pride that will not be humbled? Oh, his wounded, resentful pride writhed and twisted with the pain of it all until the focus of all the hate and all the hurt was found in *a purpose that would not be halted*, to find the man, and somehow bring him down; to bring him down to his own level, and to make him swallow those words of contempt: 'Neither will I eat bread nor drink water in this place,' making himself out to be better than the old prophet – for *he* had been eating bread and drinking water there for these years and months past. So the purpose was formulated and pursued until he found the man of God. The animosity that seared his spirit.

Tell me, are you more active against the people of God than against the enemies of God? Are you? Is it possible? Do you write more, do you talk more, do you think more, do you plan more, against the servants of God, than His enemies? Do you? I'll tell you why. Because the life of somebody has condemned you. Not directly, but implicitly. If I am speaking to some parents, does your child's love for Jesus Christ condemn your lack of love? If I am speaking to some minister, does the zeal of someone in your church condemn your lack of it? If I am speaking to some Christian worker, is your compromising with the world condemned by the consecration of your colleague; to a clerk or typist, or nurse, is your silence condemned by the witness of that new girl; to a missionary, is the standard of your devotion to Jesus Christ – or lack of it – condemned by another? Tell me, have you got a pride that will not be humbled? You go to church, but in your heart you are pursuing some devilish purpose to mar their shining example by fair means or foul, so that they, too, may come under condemnation for having dared to suggest that you, with your position, with all your experience, and of your age, that *you* were wrong? Listen, my friend, very briefly, very briefly as I close. You and I have been looking into the mirror of God's truth in the light of this 'old prophet'. We have seen the lethargy that marked his service, the animosity that seared his spirit; note also –

THE TRAGEDY THAT CROWNED HIS SUCCESS. For the old prophet succeeded. And listen: you too can succeed. Parent, you can take the love of your child for Christ, that love, that burden for souls, and *you can kill that*. Brother minister, you can dampen all the burning zeal of that young fellow and quench it. Christian worker, you can lower the standards of that other person, you can silence that fresh and artless testimony. You can. The old prophet did. And to do it, you will use *the weapon that he used*. Do you know what that was? He used his tongue. And with a blend of friendliness, a touch of authority, a suggestion of divine guidance, with his tongue the old prophet – are you listening? – he *lied*.

And as he spoke, he knew he lied. You, too, can use your tongue, one of the most powerful and deadly things we possess. That is why it is one of the touchstones of Christian maturity: 'If any man offend not in word [in tongue], the same is a perfect man.' You can go on talking persistently: you can speak authoritatively, you can even use the language of spirituality; and in the use of your tongue *you can lie*. And even as you are claiming that what you say is right, you know in your heart that you are lying.

The old prophet knew that he lied. Is there some older Christian masking these words? Are you false in your dealings with the young, whoever they are, with that other servant of God, whether flagrantly, whether obviously, or whether rather cleverly and with just a tinge of suggestion? You are a liar, and you know it. The weapon you used was the weapon the old prophet used. It was the weapon the devil used when he said to our first parents, 'Ye shall not surely die!'

The weapon he used; and *the wreckage he saw*. He brought the young man to the path of disobedience. He brought him into the place of danger. He brought him to the place of death. For suddenly, a leap from a lion, a moment of agony, and a life of usefulness was over. The tragedy that crowned his success.

You see, he did succeed. And one of the supreme tragedies of age is that when we succeed, *we kill* – somebody's love for the Master, somebody's purpose of obedience, somebody's devotion and surrender. We succeed, and we slay.

Old prophet, how many lives of usefulness have you ended? The life of one of your children? A member of your church? Somebody on the mission-station? Somebody who came under your authority? You lied, and you slew. Old prophet, is there somebody you have not killed yet, but are planning to? Come, stand for just one moment as we close by the wreckage of the life you lied to destroy. Can you see the face, as the old prophet looked on the face of the man of God on the road that day. The love you killed, the devotion you slew, the testimony you silenced, the consecration you destroyed, the usefulness you ended?

Come, stand by the old prophet. I wonder if you have one thing more in common with him? Listen, we have studied the lethargy that marred his service; the animosity that seared his spirit; the tragedy that crowned his success; can you finally share this? We see –

THE AGONY THAT BROKE HIS HEART: 'And the old prophet came to the city, to mourn. . .' Thank God for the *tears that flowed down his cheeks*! Do you know anything of tears like these? If you don't know what it is to weep here, I only hope that God will give you a place in heaven where you can weep, and weep, and weep, and weep . . . for the child of God whose usefulness you killed, whose love you extinguished. Ah, there are those alive today, but all the testimony, all the usefulness, everything worthwhile is *dead*. And it was an old prophet that did it.

If we share the agony that broke the heart of the old prophet, and know of something of the tears that flowed, then possibly we, too, may share one other thing in the agony that he knew, for we read in the story not only of the tears that flowed, but of the *truth that fell from his lips*. For at last the old prophet would seem to have been brought back to God, and the lips that had been sealed and silent for so long without any real testimony bore this testimony: 'The saying which he cried by the word of the Lord shall surely come to pass.' And if, when reading these words, you know in your heart that your experience of the past months, or even years, has been that of the old prophet that dwelt at Bethel, then may God grant that your lips too may be unsealed, and that once again a testimony to the word of the Lord may fall from your lips, bringing grace and mercy and salvation to others.

7

ELIJAH: THE DARK HOURS OF THE SOUL

'And he requested for himself that he might die'
(1 Kings 19.4).

I wonder whether there are those who can recall an hour in their lives when they have been overwhelmed with the temptation to despair, a temptation to give up, and there seemed to be no light but only darkness within? I believe that that is a true account of experience of the soul from time to time, and it may well be that God has laid this theme upon my heart because for some servant of His this is not a memory of something that happened long ago, but an accurate description of what is happening now in your spiritual experience. You, too, have reached a point where you are overwhelmed with a darkness within, and a despair, and a feeling that you want to give up.

Continually one comes across Christians who have given up: missionaries who have not returned to the field; ministers who have given up the standards which they set out in their high sense of their calling; Christians who at one time played a vital part in the life of their church. What wreckage marks the pathway of the Church of God – the wrecked lives of those who have given up, those who have dropped out, those who have found themselves lost in the darkness of despair! I want to look at this story concerning Elijah; it may be that there is someone reading these words whom God wants to lead out of the darkness into the glorious light and liberty of the children of God. First notice –

WHERE THIS IS FOUND. What are the kind of people to whom this might happen? And when is this type of thing likely to happen? Here we have almost a sense of shock and surprise, for when we consider where this dark hour of the soul is recorded, we are staggered and astonished to find that it is happening *in such a man*.

For here we are dealing with one of the spiritual giants of the Old Testament, Elijah, the man who has just achieved one of the most remarkable victories for the cause of God. The temptation to despair is rising up in the soul, not of a small or insignificant man, but of one of the great giants of God. In such a man! What an amazing thing!

Yet I wonder whether the dark hours are not more common that we think. Both Scripture and Christian biography bear ample testimony to their existence. Listen to the psalmist: 'Oh, that I had wings like a dove! For then I would fly away, and be at rest' (Psalm 55.6). There is a shadow there on the spirit. Here is a person who wants to run away. Listen to the prophet. 'Oh, that I had in the wilderness, a lodging place . . . that I might leave my people, and go from them!' (Jeremiah 9.2). Is there a prophet teaching then who is tired of the burden of his people: that mission-station, that church, that school, that hospital, that family? Listen to the preacher. Here is Jonah, who has just witnessed a great revival. What is his language? 'Therefore now, O Lord, take, I beseech Thee, my life from me; for it is better for me to die than to live.' In such a man! Yes, the dark hour of the soul is much more common than we think.

If we turn to Christian biography, listen to Sister Eva, of Friedenshort. This is how she writes: 'In myself I saw nothing but sin, incapability and weakness. I was almost too tired to speak or eat. I took my Bible and went out and laid myself down on a bed of moss.' Elijah chose a juniper tree, Sister Eva a bed of moss, but they were both in the same condition. It was for both the dark hour of the soul: and the thing that is startling and staggering is that it is found in such a man, in such a woman!

Elijah, a man whose obedience had been proved and tested right to the hilt, a man whose testimony concerning his obedience was staggering; one able to stand before

63

God, and before an apostate nation, and say that as far as God's will was concerned, 'I have done all.' There was not a thing that God required of him which he had not done. This is the quality of man we are dealing with: a man whose communion with God was as real as it could have been. 'As the Lord God liveth, before Whom I stand,' and that was no empty claim. He faced insuperable odds with unshaken confidence. He faced a drenched altar with its sodden wood and its trench swimming with water, and yet there had been no faltering in his faith. 'Hear me, O Lord, hear me, that this people may know that Thou art the Lord God.' And God heard him. Here was a man whose obedience was proven, whose communion with God was intimate, whose courage had been displayed, whose prayers were answered: and it was in the soul of such a man that darkness fell.

Where was it found? in such a man! Surprising too, because it was *at such a moment*.

When did this temptation break in upon the soul of this giant? It was at a time of unparalleled opportunity. There had been the most unmistakable evidence of God's working with him. There had been the provision of his needs by the brook of Cherith; there had been the cruse of oil that failed not; and then a final, staggering, amazing miracle, the evidence of God's presence and power, when the fire of the Lord fell, when the people bowed down and cried out, saying, 'The Lord, He is the God.'

Is your life such a life? Are you a Christian man or woman, possibly old in the service of the King, the whole testimony of your life right up to this hour bearing the evidence of God's power working with you? Not only was there this evidence of God's working with Elijah, but all around him was the experience of answered prayer. Thousands of people had been touched by God through the faithfulness of this one man. 'Hear me,' he cried, 'hear me, that this people may know. . .' And God had heard, and the people knew! Then there had come the drenching rain. At such a moment the apostasy and apathy of a nation had been challenged and broken, and the door of opportunity for God was open wider than it had been for a generation. It was at such an hour that the darkness fell. An hour of victory, an hour of opportunity; yet here is a man thinking in terms as if it had been an hour of defeat.

In such a man, at such a moment, and *over such a matter*. It was so small a matter compared with the tremendous obstacles he had overcome. The man who had faced a thousand hostile priests, the man who had dared the hatred of the whole royal court, trembles before the threat of a woman! Is it not extraordinary how sometimes the darkness can fall over such a small matter, and all of a sudden the light has gone right out of the sky?

Was it not S. D. Gordon who said once, 'You can shut out the light of the sun with a threepenny bit, if you hold it close enough to your eye'? It does not take a great deal to cloud the sun in the life of the soul. I want you to notice that it was like this in such a man, at such a moment, and over such a matter. We are dealing not in terms of pygmies, now; we are dealing in terms of giants. Elijah would not call himself that; you would not call yourself that – but others might, history will. Is there somebody reading these words going through the dark hours of the soul? That is where it is found, and it is much more common than you think.

I want you to notice, not only where it was found, but –

HOW IT WAS FOSTERED. What do we find in the thinking of this man at this hour? What condition was he in that exposed him, that endangered him, that brought for the moment the whole of his future ministry into jeopardy? There are three statements that Elijah makes which seem to me to give us an indication as to what was happening in his heart. The first is in v.4, 'Now, O Lord, take away my life; for I am not better than my fathers.'

The first thing that was fostering this darkness was a sense of *his sinfulness in the sight of God*. 'I am not better than my fathers.' Strange, is it not, that at a time when the name Elijah was on everyone's lips, praising God for what Elijah had done; when all around there was faith rekindled; when in every home there were altars rebuilt, at a time when the whole land was ringing with the story of what God had done through this man, at that very hour the man himself was wrapped up in the sense his own sinfulness. There had been failure, of course there had: he had run away.

Is this the one thing filling your heart, a sense of failure? You know that you are not better than anyone else? There may be a solid basis of fact for that! You are not imagining things: there has been failure. You feel that you are done, you are finished.

That is surely the point of danger for the Christian: when failure comes. It need not come; but if it does, what is the particular danger? Surely the danger is simply this, that we move off the ground of the grace of God! All true Christians are prepared to recognise that we are justified by grace, and then having been justified by grace we are tempted to move off that territory, and start reckoning in terms of our righteousness, our faithfulness, our goodness, our experience, our understanding, our record; we move off the ground of grace. But never for one split second does any Christian get off that ground as far as God is concerned. There is never any moment when I have any claim upon God based upon anything in myself. It is still true that all our righteousnesses are as filthy rags, even if our righteousnesses are Christian ones.

Have you moved off the ground of grace, and are you lost and discouraged and despairing because of your own sinfulness as a Christian? My friend, you will never get beyond the stage of being 'accepted in the Beloved'. Thank God for that; that there is never any moment when I am ever accepted by God because of anything in me, but simply and solely because of what is in Christ. If you start moving off the ground of grace, and start thinking that God must use you, and God has used you because of what you are, then you are exposed to danger. Saved by grace, we must stand in grace!

So this man was filled with a sense of his sinfulness in the sight of God. 'I am not better than my fathers.' But another thing fostered this darkness and that was *his loneliness in*

66

the will of God. He says, 'I, even I only, am left; and they seek my life, to take it away' (1 Kings 19.10). What a dangerous thing loneliness can be; and what a difficult thing! I wonder if this sometimes happens to missionaries, that they lose their standards because they have been so desperately lonely during the first term of their service on the field. It is so easy to let things slide when there is no one else to keep us up to the mark. It is so easy to become discouraged when there is no one to share the burden with us, to pray the thing through. It may be that we are in a church, or in a new job, and we are the only Christians there, and the thing that has fostered this dangerous spiritual situation is the loneliness of it. We have not anybody to stand alongside; nobody seems to care.

I would ask a question here of members of churches who have undertaken the responsibility of supporting and praying for those on the mission-field. When did you last write to your missionary? You might say, 'Well, I haven't much time.' But you have all the time there is! If you knew something of the desperate loneliness that overwhelms the spirit of those who are right in the forefront of the battle, you would make time to write! You said to them, 'We'll pray for you, we'll think of you,' but there is no tangible evidence of either of these things.

I wonder how many missionaries have lost out, and are not on the field now, and the fault is not theirs. The fault is that of the church at home whose members have been too lazy to care enough to pray or to write. It might mean a great deal to some desperately discouraged, lonely soul fighting temptation on the mission-field if a postcard went out tomorrow with a coloured view of home. It might be that the sense of being remembered, prayed for, cared for, might come just at the crucial moment.

Do you know that some missionaries have come home after one term of service, having gone out with all their zeal and all their love for the Lord, and trained to the hilt, consecrated to the limit, and they have come back wrecked? Whose fault? I would put nine-tenths of the blame on the church at home, that does not care. We are hypocrites when we say we do, if there is no tangible evidence of it.

But it is not only missionaries abroad who need help; it is sometimes Christians who leave home, who leave the fellowship of a living church, and find themselves desperately lonely. Elijah felt so alone, and his loneliness in the will of God was one of the things that fostered this dark hour.

His sinfulness in the sight of God, his loneliness in the will of God, and *his weariness in the work of God*. Notice how he says in v.10, 'I have been very jealous for the Lord God of hosts.' What a record of achievement this man had, what emotional stress he had endured, what physical hardship he had experienced, what spiritual results he had seen! The man was exhausted. Then the devil came in. How cleverly he times his attack! It was so with our Lord: when He had fasted forty days and forty nights, then the tempter came. And the devil will try to get in, and the darkness will begin to gather when you are at a stage of utter weariness and exhaustion, and you are thoroughly tired out.

Is there somebody reading this who is utterly weary? You have reached the end; you are not going back to the mission-field. No, not now; you are finished. You are not going to take up that Sunday-School class again; you have had enough of it. You have been teaching for two years and that is as much as you can stand; you just cannot do it, you are done. You are not continuing in that job to which God called you; it is too difficult, so you are changing. You are the only Christian there, and it has been simply impossible. You are sending in your notice. Just tired out.

Where it was found; how it was fostered, and then, finally –

HOW IT WAS FACED. For Elijah, thank God, did not finish his ministry here! He might have! It is possible that you have been making up your mind that your ministry and your witness are finished. You have come to the end of it. You are going to relax, to settle back, to become an ordinary Christian. You are giving up the fight. You have that clearly in your mind. But Elijah's ministry did not finish, although he wanted it to. Is it not a mercy that God does not answer all our prayers? 'O Lord, take away my life.' He did not, you know; He gave it back to him.

I remember reading in the life of Robert Murray M'Cheyne these lovely words: 'At the very time when I was beginning to give up in despair, God gave me tokens of His presence.' Fancy Robert Murray M'Cheyne giving up in despair! You see, the giants are in it, all of them. And if you think that you are a kind of peculiar exception because you go through dark hours when it seems that you must give up, you are not an exception; you are in very good company; I could not imagine better company than Robert M'Cheyne! I am not fit to be in that company; but it would be wonderful to be in it. 'At the very time when I was beginning to give up in despair, God gave me tokens of His presence.'

What were the tokens? Well, first there was *a very practical matter to be seen to*. This man was utterly spent and exhausted, with a body in need of attention as well as a soul; and God's way out began with sleep and food. Is that the kind of blessing you are looking for? It may be just the kind of blessing you are needing. Just a few nights' good sleep! An angel helped to deal with this. I do not think this angel had wings; not this one! Somehow or other, I think this angel was a woman, living in a croft nearby, who came out in the morning and found a sleeping man, exhausted and tired out under a tree. And do you know what she did? She went and put the kettle on! Has that anything to do with holiness, with recommissioning? Yes, it has indeed. Well, as a matter of fact, it was not a kettle, it was a cruse of oil. We had better stick to Scripture! I think she put the griddle on anyway, because she baked a cake on the coals.

Thank God for this kind of ministry. This brings a word of encouragement and cheer to some ladies who feel that their ministry is rather different from Elijah's! Well, it took an angel who could bake a cake to get this man on his feet again! And that was a pretty big day's work, was it not? You would not think a cake could do it, but it did! You would not think that two night's sound sleep could change a man, but it did.

We have to be sensible! See that you get enough sleep; and that means not so much the time you get up in the morning, as when you go to bed at night. That is when the battle begins. When I was in India I picked up the *Journal of John Wesley*. I had always been challenged, and in some measure ashamed, by the fact that some of these great giants seemed to be able to get up at a very early hour; but I noticed when I read through John Wesley's *Journal*, not only when he got up but when he went to bed – and I found that if he got up an hour or so earlier than I did, he went to bed a couple of hours sooner!

Let us then be sensible, let us be practical, let us be realistic, and let us remember that God's will is concerned not just with our souls but with our bodies. The first thing that God did to this man, who was utterly worn out, was to say, 'You need sleep and food, food and sleep. Go to bed, man.' And for some of us, the first step out of the darkness into light might be to get a bit of rest for our tired bodies.

There was not only a very practical ministry, but then came *a very personal message*, a very personal message to be listened to! 'The word of the Lord came to him.' I wonder if you noticed a very suggestive and significant phrase in that little quotation I gave you from Sister Eva: 'In myself I saw nothing but sin, incapability and weakness. I was almost too tired to speak or eat. **I took my Bible** and went out and laid myself down on a bed of moss. I was almost too tired to speak or eat.' 'The word of the Lord came to him.' If ever we needed the Word of God, it is in an hour like this. If ever you want the light of the truth of God, it is when there is darkness in your soul; and I would say that if your soul is there in the dark, then take your Bible with you, and see if the Word of the Lord does not come to you.

How unspeakably blessed it was, and how infinitely tender and gentle God was. No earthquake for Elijah, no rent mountains and rocks, no fire now – this man was beyond the reach of these things – but just a quiet voice. There was a rebuke, but it was very gentle. And a still, small voice

70

spoke. Is there a voice that wants to speak with you today? Not the voice of anger, nor the voice that will rend, but just the quiet voice of the Lord. What does He want to speak to you about? Well, *a very important mission* to be attended to. A bit of work that He has for you to do. You see, there is no discharge from the service of the King. And this man, who was running away, heard a voice saying, 'Go, return.'

Go, return, back to that station, back to that Sunday-School class, back to that shop, back to that hospital, back to that school, back to that job, back to that ward, back – go, return, go, return; there is no release, no discharge. Go back – why? Because you have not finished your work, and God has not finished with you. Do you know that there may be an Elisha waiting for your return? There may be a life waiting, a bigger work, a better work; there is a man you have not met yet, there is a life you have not seen yet. You have done well, but you will do better work yet than anything you have done. You will find Elisha, and then you will train him to work; and what you do when you go back is going to be more than you have done up to now. What will you find? You will find again the guidance of God directing your way and bringing you into touch with lives you can bless. You will find the evidence of God's power manifest. Maybe you will find a fellowship that at last ends the loneliness. But I know this: that if you do go back, you will find at the end the surprise of your life. You will find, like Elijah, that there is a reward coming that far exceeds anything you have ever thought or dreamed of.

Go, return. God's cure for this man who wanted to run away was to give him more work to do. How was it faced? The Word of the Lord came to him. It would be wonderful, would it not, if this very day you took your Bible, and if the Word of the Lord came through it, and into the darkness came the first gleam of light, and you realised suddenly that you are not cast off, you are not done yet. This is just the dark hour of the soul.

Have you ever noticed how in Psalm 23 the psalmist says, 'Yea, though I walk through the valley of darkness, I will fear no evil, for Thou art with me.' But what is a valley of

71

darkness? Surely the way from one green pasture to another: that is all. And you have been going through the dark hour. You are not alone, Christian friend, you are not alone. Giants of the faith have been there. You are found in it, but it is just the way from one pasture to another. It happens to be dark for a while, the sun has gone out of the sky; but keep close to the Shepherd, and He will lead you through and lead you out.

Is anybody wanting to die? No, God did not want Elijah to die at all; and he never did. God gave him a wonderful homecoming, when the chariot of fire came, and took the tired but faithful servant home to glory. The day will come when God will say to you, 'Now your time is up. It is time you came.' Then we shall be glad to go; and we shall be so thankful that we did not give up, that we did not drop out. Do you know the lines:

> On, bear and suffer all things;
> 'Tis but a stretch of road:
> Then, wondrous word of welcome,
> And then, the Face of God.

Wonderful welcome when we see that Face, and we realise that when the dark hour came we did not give up, but went through.

8

ELISHA: A MIRACLE OF RECOVERY

'And the man of God said, "Where fell it?" And he showed him the place' (2 Kings 6.1-7).

One of the most helpful things about the Bible, one of the things that makes the reading of it so relevant to the problems of life as we face them, is that we find reflected in its pages the experiences of our own lives today. Sometimes this may be seen in the simple statements the Bible contains; at other times it may be reflected in a more pictorial form of visual aid in the parables and in the miracles recorded there for our learning and help. I want to look with you at the miracle that is recorded in the opening verses of 2 Kings 6, and I hope we shall see there some lessons in the experience of the soul which are possibly just what we may need to learn for ourselves!

First of all we find here –

A LEADERSHIP IN THE WORK OF GOD THAT WAS THRILLING. A key word in the opening verse of the chapter is the name of a man, and that name is Elisha. Let us begin, then, by noting *the presence in their midst*.

This particular group of men, this school of the prophets, was privileged beyond all others in that at this time the leadership of the work of God was in the hands of Elisha. I have emphasised that the key word in the opening verses was the name of a man; and often in life there are times when in a special way the key to the experience of so many of us can be summed up in the name of a man.

This is true in the ordinary affairs of nations. Two names, for example, that for so many held the key to the situation in the dark war years in my country were the names of Churchill and Montgomery. But not only is this true in the ordinary affairs of nations and men, but also in the spiritual experience of Christians. It is true of the spiritual life and conditions in cities, for example; it is equally true in the story of the rise and fall of individual congregations; as well as in the spiritual experience of individual Christian people. The key word so often has been the name of a man, a man under whose leadership there has been exercised a tremendous influence for spiritual good.

It would be a fascinating study if we could pause and find out how many names have played their parts in your lives and in mine. We would have to recall and record with gratitude the enlightenment that has come to our minds by the grace of God through their words. We have been able to see in them the embodiment of the message that they preached. The name of Elisha was such an embodiment to these men long ago. How privileged we, like them, have been.

I want to note also *the prospects in their minds*. Under such leadership the talk was all of expansion, of progress. The scenes were all scenes of activity. 'Behold now the place where we dwell with thee is too straight for us. Let us go, and let us make a place where we may dwell.' The possibilities under such leadership have seemed endless. There was just no limit to what God could do or could not do.

No wonder I titled this part of our message, 'A leadership in the work of God that was thrilling'. To have met some people, to have sat under some ministries, to have worked with some men, is to have the horizons of life pushed right back and opened right out. This, we have exclaimed to ourselves, is what a Church should be. This is what the Christian life should be. This is what the Gospel of Christ can do. And as we have looked and listened to and laboured under such leadership, our hearts have begun to burn within us. A leadership in the work of God that was thrilling.

Tell me, have you not known something of this on a larger or on a smaller scale? Surely you must! Is there a name vivid in your memory just now of someone through whom, under God, your life was deeply touched and blessed, deeply challenged, and stirred and moved? Your life, too, has known what these men knew long ago: a leadership in the work of God that was thrilling.

Secondly, I want to note –

A LOSS IN THE WORK OF GOD THAT WAS TRAGIC. In the midst of all their dreams, in the midst of all they were busy doing, there came disaster to one life (2 Kings 6.5-6). Something went wrong with one man who was as busy as the rest, as much in the thick of it as all the others; one man who was 'with it' as far as Elisha was concerned. We read that suddenly the axehead flew off and was lost in the deep and muddy waters of the Jordan. The thing which had made this man's contribution effective had gone – the keen sharp cutting blade of the axe – and he was left with the useless shaft of the axe in his hand.

Tell me, is this old story not strangely and searchingly up to date? Have you not seen this happen, a Christian suddenly and strangely ceasing to count as far as all effective service is concerned? Something seems to have gone wrong in his life; something seems to have gone out of his spiritual experience, out of his testimony. There has been a loss in the work of God that has been tragic. Oh yes, we have seen it happen again and again and it could be happening in your life here and now. There are two things I want to notice concerning this loss. The first is that *it was a conscious loss*. He knew it, and I am sure that others noticed it. 'As one was felling a beam, the axehead fell into the water; and he cried and said, Alas, master! for it was borrowed.' It was a conscious loss. All spiritual effectiveness is likewise borrowed: borrowed from the God who bestowed it and who can withhold it. Spiritual power can be lost, and when it is lost we know it. We know it; yes, and others notice it.

I wonder if others have noticed that things are not well with you as once they were? Has something gone out of your prayer life, out of your testimony, out of your Christian service? I am quite certain that if it has, then one thing is true: you know it, and others have seen it. In your life, as in the life of this man long ago, the loss has been a conscious loss. He was fully aware that something had happened, that something vital had gone out of his life; that that which made his contribution to the total impact and work of the whole had disappeared.

I wonder if this is precisely the condition in which you are today? There has been in your life a leadership in the work of God that has been thrilling, but there has also been a loss in the work of God that has been tragic; and it has been a conscious loss – you know it. But it was more than a conscious loss, *it was a confessed loss*.

'And the man of God said, Where fell it? And he shewed him the place' (v.6). Elisha assumed that this man knew where he had lost his axehead. He asked the question, 'Where did it fall?' Where did you lose it? And the man showed him the place. It was a very precise question. Where? asked Elisha; and the man showed him 'the place'. Two things were called for from this man. The first was humility, and the second honesty.

I wonder if God Himself were to speak to us as precisely as Elisha did to that man, would we be willing to respond with the honesty and humility with which this man responded long ago? I wonder if you know as clearly as this man knew where the loss has occurred in your own spiritual Christian life and testimony? Has it been a neglected Word of God? Has it been a silenced voice of prayer? Has it been a sin unconfessed, unforsaken, and therefore unforgiven? Has there been a resistance to the will of God as the only authority the Christian life can accept?

'Where fell it?' Do you remember the question asked by one of our hymns, 'Where is the blessedness I knew when I first saw the Lord?' Where fell it? 'And he shewed him the place.' Will you do just that very thing today? And if you do, then you can move with us into the final lesson we can learn here from this miracle and parable of long ago.

We have seen here a leadership in the work of God that was thrilling; we have seen a loss in the work of God that was tragic; and finally, we see here –

A LIFE IN THE WORK OF GOD THAT WAS TAKEN UP AGAIN.

As I was looking at the closing events of this incident, two thoughts came to my mind. I see here, first *the impossibility of recovery*. This must surely have been in the mind of that man. The Jordan may have been in flood, the task of recovery hopeless, the river deep and the current swift and strong, the water muddy. The axehead was not only gone, it was gone for good. Was that the conviction which lay behind the cry of distress and even of despair?

Whether it was so in the case of the man or not, I know sometimes we feel like that about ourselves. We think like that about others. The story of usefulness in spiritual things has ended in tragedy, and there would seem to be no hope of any recovery at all. We might as well close the books. 'Impossible' is the word at the back of our minds. Could we ever come to love our Bibles again as we once did? Could we ever pray again as once we used to pray? Could we ever bear witness again to the saving power and the reality of Jesus Christ as once we were able to do? Could we ever again enjoy Christian fellowship as once we used to know it at a great and real and living depth? No, our heart cries out, it is impossible.

But was it not Hudson Taylor who said that whenever God does anything, we find that it is in the first place impossible, in the second place difficult, in the third place done. For though I see here the impossibility of recovery, I see more; I see *the immediacy of response*. We read, 'Elisha cut down a stick, and cast it in thither; and the iron did swim.' What had seemed gone for ever was now not only within sight, it was within reach, and all because a power greater than any human power had been at work. When God wants to bring what we have lost within sight, he too uses the wood of a tree, wet not with water, but with the blood, and that blood the blood of His own Son!

There is forgiveness for the saint as well as for the sinner in the Cross of Christ; and sometimes it is the saint who needs the message more. 'Their sins and their iniquities will I remember no more,' is the word of God. 'I have blotted out as a thick cloud thy transgressions, and as a cloud thy sins,' is the promise of the Word of God. 'Though your sins be as scarlet, they shall be as white as snow; though they be red like crimson, they shall be as wool.' 'If we confess our sins, He is faithful and just to forgive us our sins, and to cleanse us from all unrighteousness' – from *all* unrighteousness. The promise in 1 John 1.9 does *not* say 'from all unrighteousness except from some', but from *all*: and we must not and we dare not make exceptions where God makes none.

I find sometimes that it is much harder to get the Christian who has fallen tragically into sin to believe in the forgiveness of sins, than the unconverted man or woman who stumbles upon the message of the Cross for the first time. But there is forgiveness of sins for the saint, as well as for the sinner! And how much we need to claim that little word *all* as the word that covers our need. The world's forgiveness, and even the forgiveness of other Christians, is not on the same scale as God's. Sometimes Christians may forgive but they cannot forget, whereas God says, 'Their sins and their iniquities will I remember no more.' If God forgets when He forgives, why should we recall what He has for ever cast behind His back? '. . . And the iron did swim.' There, within sight and within reach, was all that he had lost; and we read, 'And Elisha said, Take it up to thee. And he put out his hand, and took it.'

I wonder whether God has laid this word upon my heart so that some Christian who has lost everything that made his Christian life and testimony effective may realise that God wants him to reach out his hand and take back what he thought he had lost for good? Will you do that even now? Put out the hand of faith and, in the light of the cleansing from sin and the forgiveness of sins that God offers through the blood of the Cross, in the light of the Cross itself and the passion of His Son, take up again the life of effective service that is God's intention for you and take your place once again in the ranks of those who have something of value to render in the fellowship of the Christian Church, to the total good of mankind and the ultimate glory of God.

This story then of long ago is the story of today! This story of a man who lived centuries ago in the far-off land of Palestine is the story of some Christian living today. It is a three-fold story. Has it been your story? A leadership in the work of God that was thrilling; a loss in the work of God that was tragic; and a life in the work of God that was taken up again.

May God grant that the happy ending of this Old Testament miracle and parable may be your experience, for Christ's sake.

9

ELISHA: THE SIN OF SILENCE

'We do not well, this day is a day of good tidings, and we
hold our peace.' (2 Kings, 7.9).

A study of the Bible reveals that very often the worst
sinners are not necessarily those who do what is wrong, but
those who fail to do what is right! Those familiar with the
Book of Common Prayer, which used to be used in every
Anglican church, will recall that in the General Confession
with which Morning and Evening Prayer always began, the
words included a confession of sins of omission *and* sins of
commission, and **began** with the first: 'We have left undone
those things which we ought to have done and we have
done those things which we ought not to have done.' 'Sin',
the Bible says, 'is the transgression of the law.' The Bible
also says that 'to him that knoweth to do good and doeth it
not to him it is sin'. Our examination of this Old Testament
miracle leads us into a study of one of the sins of omission. I
call it the sin of silence!

The story before us is a fascinating one, and challenging
too in its implications for us. The words of our text are the
words spoken by the four leprous men who had suddenly
discovered the miracle of deliverance wrought by God
which meant life, not only to them but also to those in the
beleaguered city of Samaria.

Someone has said that all great teachers teach pic-
torially, our Lord was a classical example of the art of
illustration, and many modern preachers would do well to
follow His example. It has been said that some sermons are
all door and no house, while others are all house and no
door, but it could also be said that some sermons may be

both door and house, but house with no windows, dark and a bit dreary! Miracles, which in the Bible are just parables in action, and parables themselves, which are pictures painted with words, both constitute a kind of visual aid to our understanding of the ways of God. I believe that this story before us is an excellent example of this. Let us see then what light it has to shed upon our subject, the sin of silence.

The changing moods, emotions and experiences through which the four lepers passed have a fuller meaning than lies upon the surface. For them it was 'a day of good tidings'. So, too, surely is every day for the Christian still. When the birth of Christ was announced it was in similar terms: 'Behold I bring you good tidings of great joy which shall be to all people.' One of the recent modern translations of the New Testament is titled 'Good News for Modern Man'. In a time when almost all the news is bad news it is more than time that the voice of Christian testimony rang out loud and clear. How sad it is that some preachers preach the Gospel as if it was the worst of news, in tones of almost funeral gloom, and with scarcely ever even the hint of a smile!

The historical situation was quite a simple one. Samaria was under siege, surrounded by the invading hosts of the Syrian armies. The city was in a desperate plight. Cannibalism was rife as the people were starving. These four lepers had been trapped between the enemy and the walls of the city. Their conditions was both hopeless and helpless. They were banned from the city, and to enter the camp of the Syrians meant instant death. Then suddenly all was changed because God intervened. What God did then, and what God did in the coming of Jesus Christ, and what God is still willing and able to do today, is to intervene in power. Was it not Dr. Stanley Jones who said, 'The early Christians did not spend their time moaning about what the world was coming to, but rejoiced in what had come to the world!'

First of all I want to note with you how these men were –

AMAZED AT WHAT THEY HAD FOUND. Verses 3-7 tell the story of the discovery they made that at first left them speechless with amazement. And here right away we strike a note that finds an echo in the experience of every true Christian. We love to sing the words of John Newton's hymn, 'Amazing grace, how sweet the sound', and amazing that grace most surely is!

Think first of all of *the misery in which they were found*. It was a desperate situation in which they had found themselves. They had no doubt been sleeping outside the city walls, and had awakened one morning to find themselves trapped and surrounded by the Syrian hordes. The tactics of the enemy were simple enough: they would starve the city into submission.

Are we not living in similar days when an increasing sense of hopelessness and helplessness is gripping the minds of all thinking people? Evil and violence and wickedness are rampant. And there seems to be no answer, no way out.

Not so long ago some so-called theologians, ignoring in their conceit what the Bible has to say, started talking about man having come of age, about men now being like gods! I seem to remember that that was what the devil promised to our first parents long, long ago. But we don't hear much of that kind of foolish nonsense now; the picture is too frightening. Men are behaving more and more like devils. The voice of the ordinary man talks a very different language.

Listen to the words of an American journalist: 'It seems to me that living is futile, and death the final indignity!' Listen to the words of a mother, words spoken to her minister out of the agony of her grief when the pastor called to comfort her after her only son had died: 'It's all right, its all right,' she cried. 'He's well out of this damned world.' Forgive the language, but the words are hers and not mine! Listen to another writer: 'Is this all that life amounts to? To stumble almost by mistake into a universe which clearly was not designed for life, and which to all appearance is either totally indifferent or definitely hostile to it? To stay, clinging to a fragment, a grain of sand until we are frozen off? To strut our tiny hours on our tiny stage, with the knowledge that all our aspirations are doomed to final frustration, and that all our achievements must perish with our race, and we must leave this universe as though we had never been?' As someone else once said, 'So many are crying out today in the words of a man who said to a friend, "I wish you would shine some of your light in my direction. God knows, I have run out of light!"' It was, I think, Dr. Stephen Olford who said that one of the tragedies of life in the USA was the number of teenagers who were committing suicide. Hundreds of them every year are putting an end to their lives because to them life had ceased to be worth living.

We have thought then of the misery in which these men were found, and now let us note *the mystery with which they were faced.* In their desperation these lepers rose up and went into the camp of the Syrians and we read, 'Behold, there was no man there for the Lord. . .' intervened. And by that intervention the forces which had threatened to destroy them had been scattered. Into the darkness which had filled their hearts, suddenly a light shone with a brilliance that both dazed and dazzled them. God had stepped into the situation!

So it is still with men today. When Christ was born, the ancient prophecy was fulfilled which decreed that the people who walked in darkness 'would see a great light'.

These men just could not believe their eyes. They were amazed at what God had done. The forces that had encircled and trapped them had been dispersed and defeated. Surely the whole message of the Christian enshrines the same truth. It speaks of the intervention of God in human affairs. God has acted in Christ, and through that intervention and through what God has done and still can and will do in the lives of men and women, God is at work today as well as yesterday. There is miracle here, there is mystery here, but what of that? Is not the Almighty God, the Creator of the universe, able to do what man cannot do, and cannot understand? What arrogance and conceit is this when man, who knows so very little, even only a tiny fraction of reality, then sets himself up to dictate to God what he, little man as he is, has decided that his God can and cannot do! The confidence of the Christian is in a God who can and does intervene on a massive and universal scale throughout the whole world and throughout all history, and also intervenes on the intimate and personal scale and level of the needs of the individual. This is because He is a God of love, and love is never content to stand idly by and see some need unmet. No wonder that we, too, like those leprous men of long ago, have been amazed at what we have found.

The second thing to note is that these men were –

ABSORBED WITH WHAT THEY HAD GOT. When these lepers went from tent to tent everything was theirs for the taking. Think for a moment of *their sudden enrichment*. Those who moments before had nothing at all, now had everything they wanted and needed. What did they need? Was it food? It was there in abundance. Was it drink? It was there and they could take their fill and quench their thirst. Was it dress? They could take off their rags and the pick of the camp was theirs for the taking. Was it transport? Horses and asses were there. Was it wealth? They could fill their pockets and take sackfuls of gold and silver besides. They had been paupers, now they were as rich as princes.

So too, surely, it is with Christians; in complete contradiction to the popular misconception that the Christian life is impoverished, it is incredibly enriched. Paul speaks not only of the riches of the grace of God, of the exceeding riches, but of the unsearchable riches of the grace of God in Christ! So many people seem to think that when God intervenes in our lives it is to **take from us**, when all the time the teaching of the New Testament is that the Love of God is a love that wants to **give to us**. In John 3.16 we are told that 'God so loved the world that He gave. . .' This refers supremely to the giving of God's Son to the death of the cross, but that was only the beginning of the giving of the love of God. God still loves and still gives. Is it pardon we need? Is it power we need? Is it wisdom we need? Is it love we need? Is it hope we need? Every need of the human heart can be met in Christ. We are suddenly no longer paupers, but in Him we are multi-millionaires!

But the sad thing was that the sudden enrichment of the lepers led on to *their selfish enjoyment*. In v.8 we find these men having a wonderful time, eating and drinking their fill. What they wanted they took and hid much more besides. If anyone had come up to them they would have said that they were having a wonderful time and that it was tremendous what God had done for them! All that would have been true. All that is equally true of the Christian, and it is meant to be that way. The Bible speaks of a God who 'richly giveth us all things to enjoy'. When the angel appeared to the shepherds at Bethlehem to announce the birth of the Saviour the message was, 'Behold I bring you good tidings of **great joy** which shall be to all people.' I get a little disturbed sometimes when I hear of preachers who claim to be preaching the good news of what they call the Gospel who do it with scarcely ever a smile on their faces, and in tones of extreme solemnity and almost sombre gloom. It would seem to them that the Gospel is the worst of news instead of the best.

The story is told of Rabbi Duncan, Professor of Hebrew at Edinburgh University some generations ago, that one day he was walking along Princes Street in Edinburgh, twirling his umbrella in his hand and with his face alight. Someone met him and stopped him, 'Rabbi, you look as if you have heard good news,' was the greeting. The reply from Rabbi Duncan was 'Good news! Why the best of news that Jesus came into the world to save sinners!' Good news, of course it is, then away with your glum faces! In Christ there are adequate resources for every human need, in life and in death. O Preacher, let us see a smile on your face, a light in your eye, and let us hear the song in your heart. If you want to be in the Biblical succession, then be a glad preacher of good news. 'These things have I spoken unto you,' says Jesus, 'that your joy might be full.' John writes, 'These things write we unto you that your joy might be full.'

Having travelled the world and having met people of every culture, in every conceivable variety of material condition, I am more deeply convinced than ever that the Christian life truly lived is the happiest life that anyone can ever find!

Years ago I heard Professor James S. Stewart preach his tremendous sermon on the text, 'Happy art thou oh Israel, who is like unto thee oh people saved by the Lord.' He titled his sermon, 'Why be a Christian?' and the first reason was 'Because it is a *happier* life than any other.' How right the professor was! But you may object, 'I have met people who are not Christians and yet they seem to be reasonably happy.' To which we make reply, 'Their happiness is that of a blind man who has never seen. They don't know what they are missing!' Let us be assured that God meant it to be that way. God is our Father and He loves us. Every father wants his children to experience real joy, and God all the more so. Jesus said, 'If ye being evil know how to give good gifts to your children, how much more shall your Father in heaven.'

But these four men went one step further. They had been amazed at what they had found, they had been absorbed with what they had got, and then finally we can see how they were –

ASHAMED AT WHAT THEY HAD DONE. Let us note *the sin that troubled these men*; 'We do not well, this day is a day of good tidings and we hold our peace.' The sin of silence was their sin. Is it ours too? When did you last speak to anyone about Christ? When did you last invite anybody to come to your church, assuming that your church is one worth inviting someone to? 'We do not well,' is what the Authorised Version says; the Revised Standard Version, renders it, 'We are not doing right.' They were leaving the thousands in the doomed city in their desperate plight while all the time they were enjoying themselves, leaving the others without the wonderful news that deliverance had come, leaving them to die in their misery.

We talk critically today in my country of the silent majority in the political context. I want to suggest that possibly the most grievous sin in the Church today is that of being so very largely a silent majority too! The silence is being broken, but only here and there. Not long ago I watched a programme on the TV in which Mrs. Mary Whitehouse was being interviewed. She is a well-known speaker who stands up and speaks out for righteousness! She had been criticised rather severely a few days before by a bishop of the Church of England who should have known better. Her husband shared in the TV interview and was asked what he made of the outspokenness of his wife. His remark was to the effect that he felt it tragic that she seemed to be about the only one who did speak out, and he added, 'Why did it have to be a woman?' Why do we have only one Mary Whitehouse? It is more than time that the arrogance of so many was challenged. What changes might not take place in the life of our nation, indeed of the nations, if in the spiritual and moral realm of life the silence was broken. The silence before God must be broken, and the silence before men, too! The Bible says that 'To him that knoweth to do good and doeth it not, to him it is sin.'

Dr. Paul Rees of the USA, to whose ministry I owe so much, said something that has stuck in my mind and that I quote wherever I go because to me it is one of the most challenging truths I have ever heard. He said, 'Every Christian lives at the centre of expanding circles of contact.' What a fantastic sphere of influence there is to be found in every single Christian life, and when we put all the Christians together the spiritual and moral potential is almost unimaginable. It might be a healthy discipline if each of us sat down and tried to think out how many lives we are in touch with every day, to influence either for good or ill, by what we do or by what we fail to do. You and I might well be disturbed by the raucous shouting of a drunk man, but God may be more concerned about the very respectable silence of a Christian man!

We have noted the sin that troubled these men. Let us go on finally to consider *the sight that thrilled these men*! What a thrilling sight it was to see the people coming out from that seemingly doomed city and making their way to the camp of the enemy to find their every need met. To begin with, no doubt the message of deliverance was received with doubt and suspicion, but then with faith.

Not too often is the Church privileged to see such a sight. I don't think that any of us who shared in the first Crusade by Billy Graham in England at the Harringay Stadium will ever forget the sights we saw then, of people 'getting up out of their seats' and coming forward to indicate their interest in Jesus Christ. William Hickey of the *Daily Express* recorded his own impression of the sight. Having gone to Harringay with a more than sceptical mind about the whole business, he wrote in his paper the following day how he would never forget the sound of those marching feet. He came away, he wrote, 'with my pipe clenched tightly between my teeth and with the tears streaming down my cheeks.' At the great Christian Holiday Crusade at Filey, in which I had the privilege of sharing for almost twenty-five years, we have seen similar intensely moving sights, when at the end of the Christian Service Rally held each Thursday evening, people in their hundreds have come forward to indicate their willingness to serve their Lord at any time, in any place and at any cost.

Some people criticise such crusades, I know, though I sometimes wonder what they would have had to say about the great gathering on the day of Pentecost! How desperately the Church needs, and the world needs to see God at work on a big scale. The title of a well-known religious book has always fascinated me: *Your God is too Small.* Can God not do a really big thing? What is interesting, however, is that while God unquestionably does use the big crusade, the normal way through which God works is through the witness of ordinary Christians sharing their faith with others they know. Caring for such people, praying for them, and when the right moment comes, when a bridge of mutual trust and confidence has been built up, then sharing with them the person and claims of Christ!

You will recall that when our Lord wrought the miracle which brought the dead Lazarus back to life, the record states that when he that was dead came forth he was bound about with grave-clothes, 'and his face was bound about with a napkin'. He had found life, but not liberty. And Christ's further command was, 'Loose him and let him go.' Surely what the Church of Christ needs today is a great liberation, so that the testimony of Christ is heard everywhere, and the silence is ended!

10

NEHEMIAH: THE WAY PEOPLE TALK ABOUT GOD'S WORK

'And Judah said . . . and our adversary said . . . and I said . . .' (Nehemiah 4.10, 11 and 14).

Having a mind that works very largely along the lines of three things, I remember noticing these three phrases that come in the Book of Nehemiah. They seem to me to suggest, as a title for study, 'The Way People Talk About God's Work'. We might do well to ask ourselves this question, 'What do we have to say about the work of our God?' The story in the Book of Nehemiah is the story of the rebuilding of the walls of Jerusalem under the leadership of Nehemiah. You remember that he gave up a good job in a distant land to go back to his own land, to remove the reproach of the shattered walls of Jerusalem. The task had from the first been marked by signs of the blessing of God upon it, and it was now well under way when we come to this, the fourth chapter.

Constructive building is, of course, what the work of the Church is all about. Paul, writing to the Ephesians in Chapter two, verse twenty, speaks of Christians as being built 'Upon the foundation of the apostles and prophets, Jesus Christ himself being the chief cornerstone; in whom all the building fitly framed together groweth unto a holy temple in the Lord: in whom ye also are builded together for a habitation of God through the Spirit.' St. Peter in his First Epistle writes to the Church in a similar vein, 'To whom coming as unto a living stone disallowed, indeed of men, but chosen of God and precious, ye also as living stones are built up a spiritual house.' And elsewhere in the

Epistles we get this kind of amplification of what our Lord meant when He said, 'Upon this rock I will build my church'.

But if the task in which we are asked to share is that of constructive building with living people, of course, instead of material stones, the one thing we can be quite certain about is that men's tongues will always have something to say about it. It is almost an axiom that even among strangers the pattern of conversation which may begin with the weather will then move on to the government and will end by a discussion about the Church or religion. I want us to ask ourselves not simply, 'How do people talk', but, 'How do we talk about the work of God?' Because talk about it, most of us most certainly do. What do you have to say in your conversation about the work of God in the upbuilding of His Church? Listen to the voices we hear in this chapter. We find there are three, and I believe that these three voices can still be heard. The first, I have called –

THE VOICE OF DOUBT. 'And Judah said, "The strength of the bearers of burdens is decayed, and there is much rubbish; so that we are not able to build the wall."' Here is the voice of doubt which says, 'We can't.' Do you ever hear that voice? 'We can't; we can't; I can't.' In the work of God the voice of doubt and unbelief is always to be heard. As we listen to what doubt has to say, we can note two things.

First of all, doubt is thinking of *the massiveness of the task*. We read in these verses, 'There is much rubbish.' It is this that bothers the doubters. The sheer massiveness of the task. There is so much to be cleared away and so much to be built up. But whoever said the task was not a massive one? When our Lord left behind Him a handful of men, just eleven to be precise, what kind of task did He give them? He didn't give them a parish, not a city, He gave them the world! 'Go ye into all the world,' was what He said. Now, what task could be more massive than that? But He gave it to them. Massive though it was, did these men sit back and say, 'We can't?'

91

What is wrong with being given a task which is massive in all its dimensions? The greater the task, the greater the sense and the thrill of achievement. Someone once asked why it was that Hitler and Mussolini captured the youth of their nations in their day. The answer given was that both these leaders gave the youth of their nations a programme, something specific to tackle and do! So, when you and I think of the massiveness of the task that confronts the Church, the need of the lives that are to be reached, the need of the resources that will have to be found, of the decline to be halted, of the manpower to be raised, the massiveness of the task is, indeed, something that may trouble the doubter.

The voice of doubt that holds in view the massiveness of the task also holds in view *the weariness of the men*. Some folk were getting tired, and understandably so. If you have been to the Holy Land and seen something of the size of the stones used in the construction of the walls of Jerusalem, you must have wondered how on earth they were able to lift them. Judah said, 'The strength of the bearers of the burdens is decayed,' or, is failing. Now the record doesn't say that everyone was tired, just that some were. But that was enough for the voice of doubt. 'We are not able,' the doubters said. 'We can't'. 'We are not able to build the wall'. Let's face it, they had done well. Tremendous progress had been made. We are told in v.6 that the halfway stage had been reached, because, 'the people had a mind to work'. But signs of tiredness were appearing. Some of them really were tired.

But the thing that I think is significant is this, that there are always voices who make the condition of a few the grounds for making a generalisation about everyone. Because some were tired, Judah said, 'We can't'. How often in a discussion we are told, 'Everybody is saying. . .' Whenever I hear that kind of remark I immediately want a more precise statement and I will ask, 'You say everybody. What do you mean? Tell us exactly how many.' And when you get down to it and boil the whole thing down to hard facts, so often you find that maybe six or ten or twenty out

92

of hundreds are being quoted as representing 'everybody'. But the voice of doubt will take the condition of a few and the opinion of a few and generalise and impose it upon the whole situation.

Tiredness, of course, can be dangerous. To a tired man the small things can become big things. And the task that is already massive enough becomes impossibly large. And so we will hear the voice of doubt. But let us not make the weariness of others an excuse for our own indolence and don't let our voice be the voice of doubt which says, 'We can't'. As we look at the challenge of the work confronting the church today, is this our voice? We can't, and so we don't. We don't even try.

But there was another voice heard. In v. 11 we read: 'And our adversaries said.' I call this not the voice of doubt which says, 'We can't', but –

THE VOICE OF HATE which says, 'You won't'. You say, 'The voice of hate?' Yes, I say, 'The voice of hate.' Our Lord said that we would be hated! Let's face it. Goodness is not popular. The only man who lived a perfect life of goodness, of truth, of love, was found so unacceptable that men murdered him. They just couldn't stand him. And if you and I are going to be involved in the work of Jesus Christ we will find that there are adversaries and that their voice is sometimes the voice of hate. Remember what Jesus said: 'If the world hate you, you know that it hated me before it hated you. If ye were of the world, the world would love his own. But because ye are not of the world, but I have chosen you out of the world, therefore, the world hateth you.' It's not a popular thing to be a Christian. And if you want to be socially acceptable, hail fellow, well met with everybody, then you had better give up any idea of being true to Jesus Christ. You remember what St. John said: 'The friendship of the world is enmity with God!'

Here the opposition was led by Sanballat. Now, he wasn't a heathen; he was a Samaritan, half Jew. The Samaritans were a mixture, racially and religiously. Some think that Sanballat was possibly governor of Samaria and that he had ambitions to become governor of Jerusalem and was now seeing his ambition foiled by the arrival of Nehemiah with authority from the Emperor to rebuild the walls. We read, also in v.7, of an unholy alliance with the Arabians, the Ammonites and the Ashdodites. The Samaritans were, as we know, despised and hated by the Jews because of their mixture racially and their adulterously mixed-up religion. Nehemiah had no place for them. He said in Chapter 2, v.20, 'Ye have no portion nor rights nor memorial in Jerusalem.' That was his verdict. These were the people who did everything to hinder the work, the Voice of Hate! What did this voice say? It said in v.11, 'They shall not, they won't.' The Voice of Doubt says, we can't, and the Voice of Hate says, you won't.

Note, first of all, *how vicious was the way in which they talked*. 'They shall not know, neither see, till we come in the midst of them and slay them and cause the work to cease.' That was their objective. They wanted to cause the work to cease. Nothing would give them more pleasure than that. Here were people relentlessly and ruthlessly opposed to the work of God and determined by hook or by crook to bring it to a halt. I believe there are such forces in existence today; philosophies, politically-minded, socially-minded, intellectually-based, financial interests, and if there is anything that they hate it is the work of God and the Church of Jesus Christ. And the tragedy is that those who are right outside the Church get allied with those who are half in and half out like the Samaritans. Somebody said the devil isn't just fighting the Church today, he is joining it! Remember how in the time of our Lord we read a very significant sentence. We find in the story of His trial that, 'Pilate and Herod were made friends'. What an alliance that was! Pilot and Herod, a Roman and a Jew? How vicious was the way in which they talked! We want to cause this work to cease, they said.

And, also note *how various were the ways in which they worked*. There is no time to go into this in detail, but look back and read on! In Chapter 2, v.10, we read how grieved they were at what was happening, that somebody had

94

come: 'It grieved them exceedingly that there was come a man to seek the welfare of the children of Israel.' In Chapter 2, v.19, we read that they ridiculed the whole business: 'They laughed us to scorn and despised us and said, What is this thing that ye do? Will ye rebel against the King?' Ridicule and scorn are found again in v.1 of this chapter. And anger! We read that 'When Sanballat heard that we builded the wall, he was wroth.' They tried anger and they tried violence. In v.8 of Chapter 4, we read that they 'Conspired all of them together to come and to fight against Jerusalem, and to hinder it.'

In Chapter 6, verse 2, they tried friendliness, for we read, 'Sanballat and Geshem sent unto me saying, "Come let us meet together in some one of the villages in the plain of Ono." But they thought to do me mischief.' That friendly approach was met with those tremendous words of Nehemiah, 'I am doing a great work so that I cannot come down. Why shall the work cease whilst I leave it and come down to you?'

Then in Chapter 6, v.5, we find them writing letters; letters that were full of lies, and all of us engaged in God's Work know what it is to receive letters.

Before I became a minister in one of my churches, I remember getting a letter that was not signed. The writer told me that if ever I thought I was going to become a minister of that church, I had better think again. On another occasion when I was speaking at Keswick, and I can never quite understand why it is that I have been called to speak there for so many years, I remember getting another letter, also unsigned, saying that until I changed my way of preaching God would never bless what I had to say! I think it was Dr. Sangster, who, on one occasion, told of how he, too, had received an anonymous letter. It just had one word on it, and the word was 'Fool'. Dr. Sangster held the letter up and read the word in it and made this comment, 'It is the first time I have ever received a letter which had no message, but only a signature!' So the enemies of God tried every way and every device failed and the work went on. At the top of my Bible, I find the words:

'Nehemiah prayeth and continueth the work.' Isn't that lovely? Nehemiah prayed and continued in spite of the Voice of Hate that said, 'You won't'. So we have heard the Voice of Doubt and we have heard the Voice of Hate. But there was one more voice to be heard –

THE VOICE OF TRUST. The Voice of Doubt says, 'We can't', and the Voice of Hate says, 'You won't,' and the Voice of Trust says, 'God Will'. The Voice of Trust, or if you like it, The Voice of Faith! That's a lovely voice to hear when we are talking about the work of God. The voice that says, 'God will'. What did it have to say, then? We find that in Chapter 4, v.20: 'God will fight for us.'

I can only point to two facets of this Voice of Trust, firstly, *the inspiration of their faith*. We get that in v.14 in one simple phrase, 'Remember the Lord'. 'Therefore set I in the lower places behind the wall, and on the higher places, I even set the people after their families with their swords, their spears, and their bows. And I looked, and rose up, and said unto the nobles, and to the rulers, and to the rest of the people, Be not ye afraid of them: remember the Lord.'

All of the evidences of His power lay before them in the history of their nation: all the promises of His grace, all the covenants into which He had entered. They were to remember the Lord!

How easily we forget Him in the councils of the Church at large. I remember talking with someone not long ago and looking out over the condition of our own Church, our own land, parish after parish being linked up, vicarages and manses being sold, churches shut down. I remember this person saying, 'What are we going to do if revival comes and we haven't got the churches, we haven't got the buildings.' Remember the Lord.

That is what faith says. Remember the Lord. We are looking so often at ourselves, at our problems, that we are not looking to our God. Remember the Lord and His good hand upon us. That is where the inspiration of faith is to be found. In the Lord. His promises, His purposes, His provision. There are such tremendous prayers we pray in our hymns. The promise of power given to the Church by the ascending Lord was linked with the promise of the presence of the Holy Spirit to be given to them to dwell in them. And in one of our hymns of invocation concerning the Holy Spirit, we sing, 'Oh, Come, Great Spirit, Come'. Do we really want Him to come? Do we believe that He will come? Do we think in terms of the difference that His coming will really make? There is the inspiration of faith, in the Lord. And this leads, of course, on to what I have called *the vindication of their faith*.

The voice of faith and trust had said, 'God will', and God did. I love the way in which the record reads and ends in Chapter 6, v. 15-16: 'So the wall was finished. And it came to pass, that when all our enemies had heard thereof, and all the heathen that were about us saw these things, they were much cast down in their own eyes: for they perceived [and this is the tremendous sentence] that this work was wrought of God!' Trust and faith do not mean idleness. These people went on toiling. They went on sweating. They went on working. They went on watching. They went on praying, and the enabling, the protecting, the inspiring grace of God rested upon all that they did. So the wall was finished and the final verdict was clear: 'This work was wrought of our God.' And what better or truer word could have been said than that. And if it is not the work of our God, then it is not work worth doing. The Voice of Doubt said, 'We can't'. The Voice of Hate said, 'You won't', and the Voice of Trust said, 'God will'.

I want to ask you one question as I ask it of myself. Which voice is your voice? The voice of doubt, taking the condition of the few and making that a generalisation applying to everyone? The voice of hate – 'You won't' – how viciously they talked and how deviously they worked.' Or the voice of trust that says, 'God will'. God *will* fill our churches; God *will* transform our lives, God *will*, and He did. Those who had had nothing to do with the work were ashamed! They had to acknowledge that the work was the work of God. Are you on the job? God, alone, knows what the future is going to hold. Are we in the thick of the work for God? How are we talking about it? We can't, you won't, God will – may God grant that every single one of us may be saying deep down in our hearts as we go forward into whatever the future may hold, 'God will', and then find that 'God does'.

11

GOD'S REMEDY FOR MAN'S LONELINESS

'He took me from a lonesome pit. . .'

(Psalm 40.2 [Moffatt]).

Someone has said that while there is only one way to God, that is through Christ, there are a thousand ways to Christ! Again and again men and women were drawn to Christ because of widely varying and differing needs. Ultimately it is in the Cross of Christ that man's deepest need is met, but men are drawn to Him because they sense that in Him other needs too are met. I want to examine with you how in Christ one of man's deeper needs is met in a most wonderful way, and that is a need which today is becoming increasingly a problem which for so many defies solution, and this is the problem of loneliness. Some time ago a teenager was found in one of the parks in Sydney, Australia. She was high on drugs and communication was impossible. She was taken to a hospital, and just in case she came round and had something to say, a piece of paper and a pencil were left by her bedside. Later on, when a nurse looked in she found one word written on the paper, 'Lonely'.

I want to begin by noting what I call –

THE REALITY OF HUMAN LONELINESS. Let us face *the fact it is*. It is not often that I find myself disagreeing with a fellow speaker at the Keswick Convention in England, but one year one of the speakers took his text not from the Bible, with which I would not dare to disagree, but from the writings of a well-known author who had written these words, 'MEN ARE NOT ISLANDS'! Well, I knew what was implied by these words, and the truth that would be suggested by them, and the valid points which would be deduced from them, but I found myself immediately recalling the words of another writer who had said precisely the opposite. The writer was George Eliot, and in one of her letters to a Mrs. Bray she had written, 'We are all islands, each in his hidden sphere of joy or woe our hermit spirits dwell and roam apart.' I owed the discovery of that statement to the late Dr. F. W. Boreham. He quotes also from the writings of Amiel who in his journal expresses a similar sentiment, 'In all the chief matters of life we are alone, we dream alone, we suffer alone, we die alone!' I could add the witness of a great preacher, Dr. Alexander Maclaren who puts it this way: 'There is nothing more solemn than that awful loneliness in which each soul of man lives. We stretch out our hands and grasp live hands, and yet there is a universe between the two that are nearest and most truly one!' If you also want the witness of a distinguished theologian, here is what the late Professor Daniel Lamont of New College, Edinburgh, had to say. He writes: 'Perhaps it does not often happen that two persons can afford to reveal themselves entirely to each other, but even when it does happen, the attempt to do so can only partially succeed; human solitariness is as much a fact as human fellowship!' No, Mr. Preacher at Keswick, we disagree, we **are** all islands! The fact that this is so is the first point that we note.

The second point to note is *the form it takes*. This may differ from life to life with varying and changing circumstances and temperaments. There is of course a purely *physical* sense in which we can be lonely. We may live alone. Sometimes that is the lot of those getting older, when death takes away one after another of our own generation until we are left alone. Nobody ever seems to call, no one ever seems to want to write, and no one ever seems to want our company! But it can also be the lot of those who are still young; maybe we have to move from home and find ourselves living in digs or in a hostel among strangers. We can walk the streets crowded with people and yet feel desperately alone. We find ourselves in a crowd and not of it, where everyone else seems to have a friend, where there is a hubbub of conversation going on all around, and the lonely soul, with no one to speak to, is all the more lonely!

There is of course another kind of loneliness which is not so much physical as *emotional*, rooted in some experience through which we are passing that seems to isolate us from everyone else. It may be the sorrows of bereavement. It could be a time of utter bewilderment which, blended with an innate shyness, makes it impossible for us to share it with anyone else; we have found ourselves baffled by the pressures and tensions of life; there are so many questions to which we do not know the answers, questions about life, about death, about sex, about God, or even about ourselves. It could be some experience of moral defilement, and surely there is nothing so isolating as a sense of moral failure, nothing so much my own as my sin, and the shame of it, the guilt of it!

There is another kind of loneliness that we might call *spiritual*. Malcolm Muggeridge speaks of this in an interview with Roy Trevivian recorded and written about in his book *Jesus Rediscovered*. Malcolm says, 'I can trace in myself when I look back, another strain, that was a feeling I always had as a child and have now, of being a stranger in this world, of not being a native. I can remember it so vividly as almost the first recollection of life, an overpowering feeling that this world is not a place where I really belong. I recall the inconceivable poignancy with which I first heard in a passage from the Bible, the phrase 'a stranger in a strange land'. This sense that man does not belong here, because his soul belongs to eternity whereas this is a place of time and bodies.' Paul echoes this when he speaks of our citizenship being in heaven. Dr. W. E. Sangster, the great Methodist preacher, has this in mind when he speaks of 'the home-sickness of the soul'. Whatever form it may take, loneliness is a fact we have to face, and constitutes a problem too often man cannot solve.

The second aspect of this loneliness centres round what I would want to call –

THE TRAGEDY OF HUMAN LONELINESS. The tragedy is a twofold one, and the first tragic aspect of loneliness lies in *the burdens of life that we have to bear alone*. Man is both a social being and a spiritual being. He has not been meant or been created to live alone, but rather in a relationship not only with his fellow man, but with his creator God. In Genesis 2.18 we read the Divine pronouncement: 'It is not good that man should be alone.' So in differing degrees of depth, of affection and of affinity, man is meant to have fellowship, companionship both with his fellow man and His God. Loneliness is the reversal of the Divine intention, and becomes unbearable in the inability of man to bear the burdens of life alone.

Some years ago I heard Dr. Paul Rees tell of a vase of flowers being found on the parapet of a high ridge between Nice and Cannes in the South of France. It marked the spot where a wealthy girl had driven up in her sports car, and, carrying her dog in her arms, had leapt to her death, leaving behind a note which said: 'Nobody loves me but my dog, there is no peace.' It was in the same address that Dr. Rees went on to speak of a teenage boy who had run away from home, leaving behind him a note which read: 'I've gone looking for someone who has got time to listen to me. I have got so many things I want to tell.' Yes, the tragedy of loneliness lies partly in the fact that there are burdens we have to bear alone.

But, in addition, the tragedy lies in the fact that there are also *the blessings in life that we cannot share with others!* There is an old saying which we have all proved to be true that 'Sorrows shared are sorrows halved, and that joys shared are joys doubled'. The tragedy of loneliness reverses these experiences and we find our burdens and sorrows are doubled, and our joys halved!

In my life I have had the privilege and pleasure of travelling very widely all over the world, but in those journeys, although I have had some very wonderful experiences, there has been a tinge of sadness because almost always I have had to travel alone, my wife has not been able to come with me. The invitation, very understandably, has been for me alone! How different all these experiences and travels would have been if she had been able to share them with me, and I had been able to share them with her.

One of the memories of my childhood was to hear my Father recall some of his great exploits as a cricketer; he captained the school 1st XI and the University 1st XI, the latter for three successive years! But he always used to add that the real joy was when he got back home and was able to tell his old Father how well he had done, and to sense the joy and pleasure his own success brought to the heart of his Father. To have someone with us who reacts sensitively and sensibly to all that we have to say is one of the greatest gifts and greatest happinesses that life can give to us! But not to have someone like that, not to have someone with whom anything and everything can be shared in depth, to be alone, sometimes makes life itself hardly worth living! Someone said somewhere that 'everyone needs someone to love and someone to be loved by'.

The final thought we must consider is –

THE REMEDY FOR HUMAN LONELINESS. The psalmist gives us the clue we need. It is to be found in the grace and goodness of God. '*He* lifted me from a lonesome pit.' Loneliness is something that the Christian need never know, because it is something that God in His mercy and love can and will end. And the answer is a twofold one:–

Think of *the presence I can have of my Lord*. The heart of the Christian experience is the presence of the living and risen Lord dwelling in our hearts and lives by His Spirit. 'I live,' wrote St. Paul to the Galatian Church, 'yet no longer I myself, but Christ liveth in me.' The Christ of the Christian is no remote figure in history or in heaven, but a Christ living in the Christian, here and now! He is living there because He has been invited there! There is a chorus that used to be very popular which puts this truth so very clearly.

He lives! He lives! Christ Jesus lives today,
He walks with me, He talks with me along life's narrow way.

He lives! He lives! Salvation to impart.
You ask me how I know He lives, He lives within my heart!

Paul writing to the Church of Rome speaks of our being 'reconciled to God through the death of His Son,' to which he adds, 'much more then being reconciled we shall be saved by His life.' When Christ comes into our lives He brings so much more than pardon with Him, He comes Himself and all that He is and has now becomes in the deepest possible way mine, and me! Is my loneliness physical? Then He is there and I am never alone. 'Lo I am with you always', was His promise. Is my loneliness emotional? Then He understands. We are told that 'He was tempted [or tested] in all points like as we are'. Part of the significance of the incarnation is that we know now, beyond any shadow of doubt, that we have a Saviour Who knows and understands, because He has been here and has experienced all the trials and pressures of a human life. Is our emotion one of sorrow? Then He can give us hope. Is our emotion one of bewilderment, then He is the light of the world and we can experience the promise He gave which adds, 'He that followeth Me shall not walk in darkness but shall have the light of life.' In Him we will find the truth we need and the wisdom we need. Is our emotion one of defilement, then in Him we can find cleansing 'from all unrighteousness'. How assuring are the words of the hymn-writer:

> The kind but searching glance can scan
> The very wounds that shame would hide.

Is our emotion that spiritual one of feeling that somehow we don't really belong here? He will confirm us in that and at the same time tell us beyond any shadow of doubt that He has gone 'to prepare a place for us'. And so the final loneliness of what we call death, even that will be banished, for when we walk through the valley of the shadow of death we too will fear no evil, 'for Thou art with me'.

But added to the presence I can have of my Lord will be

the people I can have in my life. We want not simply Divine company, wonderful as that is, we are human, and we want human company and that we can have too! The Christian need never live his life in isolation. Dr. Sangster used to maintain that 'Christians are artists in the art of friendship'. In the book of the Acts one of the first things we are told about the early Christians is that 'all that believed were together'. They came together physically because they were together spiritually. And as it was then, so it has been ever since. The fact of Christian fellowship is one of the wonderful things about becoming a Christian. We are born again of the Spirit of God into the family of God. We now have brothers and sisters beyond calculation. Someone put it this way: 'God has no only children!' But beyond these people whom we can have in our lives who are Christians, are the others, those whom God intends us to reach with the message of His saving grace, those who through the witness of our lives and our lips He will seek to bring to Himself. As long as we have eyes to see, lips to speak and to pray, hearts to care, and, above all else, the Spirit to work through us in power, there will always be other people in our lives.

How different it is so often in the world! Sometimes we are tempted to cast envious eyes upon those who seem to have reached the top in terms of popularity in, say, show-business; their lives are full of people! But it is not always as it may seem. I remember reading the words of Shirley Bassey, who said this about her career: 'If it all ended, I would be surprised if I had even a handful of real friends!' How incredibly different the life of a lady living in Australia upon whose heart God laid a burden for girls coming out of prison who were desperately in need of help! Talking to a friend towards the end of her life, she told him how wonderful it was to look back over the years and to realise that there were now over 1,500 Christian women who had gone into full-time Christian service, whom she had first met outside a prison gate! The people that we can have in our lives! No Christian need ever be lonely, for these two reasons: the first because of the presence I can have of my

Lord, and the second, because of the people I can have in my life.

'He took me up also out of a lonesome pit.' Are you lonely? Then the Bible would say God never meant you to be lonely, and God is waiting, if you will let Him, to end that loneliness and fill your life, not only with His own gracious presence, but with many, many other lives that He is waiting to bless through you, with your distinctive personality and gifts, people that He can bless through none other.

I wonder how many remember the last Christmas broadcast of the late King George VI. I have a feeling that he knew what at that time we, his subjects, did not know, that soon he would be facing that final loneliness which we call death. He ended his Christmas broadcast with those memorable and meaningful words:

'I said to the Man who stood at the gate of the Year, "Give me a light that I may tread safely into the unknown." And He replied, "Go out into the darkness and put thine hand into the hand of God, that shall be to thee better than light and safer than a known way."' Will you do just that and find that God in a wonderful way will end your loneliness for time and for eternity.

12

THE GARDEN OF THE SOUL

'Let my Beloved come into His garden'
(Song of Solomon 4.16).

There comes a time in the lives of most of us who profess and call ourselves Christians when we do well to ask ourselves, 'What kind of a Christian am I? Am I the kind of Christian that God wants me to be, that God has made it possible for me to be? Am I the kind of Christian that the world needs me to be?' The value of Christian conventions such as those held at Keswick in the English Lake District and other similar 'deeper life' conventions, as they are sometimes called, is that they afford an opportunity to do just that! But we need some kind of standard of measurement which will enable us to ask and answer that question intelligently and biblically. I want to take the words of our text, which comes from one of the more difficult books of the Bible, in which the Bridegroom calls His Bride 'His garden' in chapter 5 v.1, and in which in return the Bride calls herself 'His garden'! Saints all down the centuries have seen in this book a picture, a parable, of the love relationship between Christ, the Heavenly Bridegroom of the New Testament, and the Church, His Bride. Let us then take the words of our text, words of invitation, 'Let my Beloved come into His garden,' and think through their implications for ourselves.

It may be that since I have retired from the parish ministry and have settled down in the country where the cottage in which we now live is surrounded by a garden, I am more aware of the lessons to be learned from our text. I want to share with you three very simple thoughts, which at the same time are deeply searching. –

In the first place let us think about –

THE INTENTION THE GARDEN REVEALS. In the first place a garden is intended to be *attractive*. We expect a garden to be beautiful, beautiful in colour and in design. One of the things that thrills us whenever we have friends coming to our new home and are taken to see the garden, is that they almost always comment, 'How beautiful it is'. I wonder if we have ever stopped to think through the truth that attractiveness is part at least, and a very important part, of the intention of God for our lives. Dr. Graham Scroggie in one of his books has a devastating sentence which reads: 'There is so much awkward piety, so much blundering goodness, so much unattractive sanctity' – unattractive sanctity!

The Bible has a lot to say about loveliness in living; it is worth repeating what has been said elsewhere. In Psalm 149 we read in the Authorised Version, that God 'will beautify the meek with salvation'. In Isaiah 61.3 part at least of the messianic mission was to give 'beauty for ashes'. In the Psalms comes the prayer: 'Let the beauty of the Lord our God be upon us,' and there too we face the command that we are to 'worship the Lord in the beauty of holiness'. We are meant to live attractive and beautiful lives. Christians ought to be lovely people to look at and to live with. The question we have to ask is, is that intention being fulfilled?

How and why this is so is simply because sin is always ugly. Name any sin you like and there is nothing beautiful about it, so if the purpose of the Saviour is to 'save His people from their sins', then surely this means that He will be taking the ugly things out of our lives, our attitudes and our relationships, and will be letting 'the beauty of the Lord our God', Who indwells us by His spirit, shine out! Christian lives, Christian homes, ought to be beautiful. Is there anything more needful in the world today than this? How often we have found ourselves being compelled to stop and admire a garden. 'How beautiful', we say to one another. Do we ever say that about Christian people, do they ever say it about us?

In the second place a garden is meant to be *productive*. In any garden the result of all the work entailed will be a wealth of colour, of fragrance, of flowers and of fruit. So much there will be the result of the hard work that someone has put into the garden, so much that would not otherwise have been there at all. It just doesn't happen by chance. A garden is meant to be productive. So, too, is the Christian life.

There are two senses in which the word 'fruit' is used about the Christian life in the New Testament. In Galatians 5.22-23 we read Paul's description of the 'fruit of the Spirit' which is 'love, joy, peace, longsuffering, gentleness, goodness, faithfulness, meekness and self-control'. Here the fruit of the Spirit is obviously referring to character, to the fact that, if the Holy Spirit is free to do in our lives what He has been given to do, and what He wants to do, the result will be the reproduction in our lives of these qualities of character which reflect, we could even dare to say, the very nature of Christ Himself.

But in a different place it would seem that the word 'fruit' has another meaning, where the creative work of the Spirit of God will not only be seen in what He does **in** us, but in what He does **through** us in the lives of others. It is in this sense that Dr. Campbell Morgan suggests that we are to understand the words of our Lord in John 15.16, where He says to His own disciples, 'Ye have not chosen Me but I have chosen you and ordained you [located you where you are] that ye should go and bring forth fruit and that your fruit should remain.'

To our first parents in the Garden of Eden came the word of God, 'Be fruitful and multiply' (Genesis 1.28). That productiveness, or more precisely re-productiveness which is characteristic of natural and physical life, is to be characteristic of spiritual life, the new life that every Christian possesses. As someone once put it: 'The fruit of a cat is a kitten!' The fruit then of a Christian is another Christian!

The promise of the presence and power of the Holy Spirit given by our Lord on the mount of the Ascension was linked with the task of being witnesses to Him to the uttermost part of the earth, and surely the purpose of that power in that witness was that others should be quickened into newness of life too! Your life and my life, are intended to be both attractive and productive. 'Let my Beloved come into His garden.'

Another lesson that we can learn has to do with, what I have called –

THE INSPECTION THE GARDEN DEMANDS. One of our daily rituals, when we are at home, takes place at the close of the day when my wife and I very frequently take a walk round the garden. We go round the garden, upon what I think we would call a tour of inspection! It is surely a wise thing to do. And this is part at least of the value of the opportunity of setting aside some time when we can make the invitation that our text suggests, not to inspect our gardens ourselves, but rather that He might inspect His garden for Himself – 'Let my Beloved come into His garden.' What does such a tour of inspection entail?

Such an inspection will concern itself with *the progress that should be seen*. So much work will have been put into the garden so there should be something to show for it. There will have been seeds planted, plants placed here and there, there will be shrubs, bushes and trees, and the gardener will want to know how they are doing, what progress will there have been. Some may be doing well, others may not. So there is the thought of progress in his mind, progress and development and growth.

Is this something that is happening in our spiritual experience as Christians? In 1 Peter 2.2 Peter writes: 'As newborn babes desire the sincere milk of the word *that ye may grow* thereby.' 'That ye may grow'. I wonder if we, as Christians, ever take time to assess our growth and development. Is there growth in our understanding of the Word of God, of the mind of God, of the ways of God. Has there been growth not only in what we are able to under-

110

stand, but in what we are able to undertake? When we were children we could neither understand nor undertake what we have been able to understand and undertake since we have come to maturity. When Paul wrote his letter to the Christians at Corinth he described them as being still 'babes', and because of that there were things that they were 'not able' to understand. Surely every home with children has had a measurement on some wall somewhere in the house where the heights of the children have been recorded as they have been growing. Surely then those too who have been born again of the Spirit should show signs of progress. But do we?

Such an inspection will also be concerned with *the problems that must be solved*. What garden does not have its problems, what Christian, what church? There are the weeds of various kinds that have to be dealt with, the nettles that sting, the bindweed that strangles. While there has been much that has had to be put into the garden, there will also be much that has to be taken out! There is always both a positive and a negative side to the will of God and the way of holiness. But there may well be different problems. Here is a plant that has been damaged (has the neighbour's cat been in the garden?). Here the storm of the previous night has left its trail of destruction; there will be shrubs that need to be tied up to a stake to give them support. Here the pruning knife will have to be applied to remove surplus wood that is absorbing an uncalled for amount of strength of the plant; here is a plant needing some extra nourishment or water. Another does not seem to suit the environment in which it has been placed, it will have to be transplanted to another part of the garden where there may be more sunshine!

As with the garden so with the soul, there are as many problems as there are personalities, as there are different circumstances. What problems there are, and we are foolish indeed if we leave them unresolved and without due care and attention. 'Let my Beloved come into His garden', is a wise invitation, and if the inspection takes time, it is time well spent. It may well save a great deal of time later

111

on. An old gardener once said to me about the danger of failing to keep the weeds down, and of letting them grow and go to seed, that 'one year's seeding would lead to seven years' weeding!' and what can happen in the soil can happen in the soul!

We have thought of the intention the garden reveals and the inspection that the garden demands. There is just one final thought which has come to me and it concerns –

THE IMPRESSION THE GARDEN CREATES. We close with two aspects to this, and the first has to do with *the delight a garden can become*. It can become a delight to those to whom the garden belongs, and also to those who may come to it and view its beauty and share in its produce. I recall the words spoken by God the Father concerning Jesus Christ His Son in Matthew 3.17, 'This is my well-beloved Son, in Whom I am well-pleased', or the words recorded in Hebrews 11.5, words spoken of Enoch, the man who walked with God, 'He had this testimony that he pleased God.'

In the light of all that God has done for us, all that God has given to us, do we have this testimony? Are our lives giving delight and pleasure to others, and, above all, to God?

Several years ago when I was given the responsibility of giving the opening address at the Keswick Convention, I felt led to title what I had to say as 'Living under the constant judgement of Love'. That love was of course God's love, and I based what I had to say upon the words of St. Paul in 1 Corinthians 4.3-4. 'With me it is a very small thing that I should be judged of you, or of man's judgement, yea, I judge not mine own self, but He that judgeth me is the Lord.' Love's judgment is the most kindly and yet the most critical judgment to which we are ever exposed! That judgment is not negative but positive, not trying to find out what is wrong for the sake of finding fault, but trying to put right anything that may be wrong, because love is always longing for the highest and the best for those it loves! When that is achieved, then love's cup of joy is filled. There is a perfection that love always longs for for those it loves. There is then the delight a garden can become, but there is just one more aspect we have to note.

There is *the desire a garden can create*; and that desire is the desire in the hearts of others to create a similar garden, to reach a similar standard of achievement! There can be a healthy envy created! I often find myself thinking over the words of Ruth to her mother-in-law, Naomi. You may recall how Naomi was resolved to return to her native land after she had lost both her husband and her two sons. She had spent many years in the land of Moab, but now she must return. She was preparing to say goodbye to her two daughters-in-law, Orpah and Ruth. But while Orpah was willing to part, Ruth was not. Those years in close touch with her mother-in-law had created a desire in her heart to know the secret of Naomi's life, and she expressed that desire in the most moving words ever written about that relationship, ending with the words, 'and Thy God shall be my God'.

When you and I have reached the stage where people are beginning to talk and think like that about us, we shall be beginning to show just what it means to be the kind of Christians that surely we are meant to be and that must be well-pleasing to our God. When people are wishing, 'I want a God Who can do for me what your God has done for you', then and only then shall we begin to feel and know that our life is the kind of life that God wants it to be.

There is a charming story told about the late Dean Ramsay, a very well-known and distinguished churchman who lived in Edinburgh many years ago. In his days afternoon tea was an established custom in certain social circles. The Dean was, it so happened, a great lover of roses, and specialised in cultivating them in his garden. It was said that if guests who had had afternoon teas with the Dean were deemed to have made the grade as far as acceptance with him was concerned, they would be asked when tea was over and they were about to depart, 'Please will you come into my garden and see my roses'. On one occasion however, so the story goes, one lady had so overwhelmed the Dean with her grace, her charm and her beauty, that when the time came for her to leave, the Dean did not say to her, 'Please will you come into my garden and see my roses,' but, instead, said, 'Please will you come into my garden and *let my roses see you*!' I wonder if the Lord would ever want to say that about you, or about me. *There* is a standard against which we can measure ourselves when we think of the intention the garden will reveal, the inspection the garden will demand, and the impression the garden will create.

13

ISAIAH: AMONG THE HILLS

'I will make all my mountains a way' (Isaiah 49.11).

This text is to me one of the loveliest that we find in the Old Testament, where God promises, 'I will make all my mountains a way', or as Moffat translates it, 'I will make a highroad of the hills'.

Those of us who live in Britain are no strangers to the hills. We have found ourselves among the mountains of the English Lake District, which were sometimes lost to view, hidden by the clouds and by the driving rain; but at other times, standing out in all their exquisite beauty with their pastel colouring that which is so distinctive of the Lakeland fells, in all the soft loveliness of sunshine and shadow. In Scotland we are not strangers to the hills, nor in Wales either, or in Ireland where the mountains of Mourne sweep down to the sea.

Those of us who are Christians are not strangers to the hills either, and that is our theme in the light of our text and of the promise of God in it, that He 'will make all my mountains a way'.

In the first place, I want us to note that our text speaks of what I would call –

THE MOUNTAIN PATH. Are there not times when our Christian experience has a great deal in common with the tracks that we have found among the hills? John Bunyan was wise and right to include both the Hill Difficulty and the Delectable Mountains in the journey of Christian from the City of Destruction to the Celestial City. We have surely all known something about the mountain-track experiences in life.

Think for a moment of *the stillness that we find among the hills*. There is a loneliness, there is a solitude to be found among the mountains. I am sure that you, like I myself, have sometimes stood still on some moorland or mountain path, looking over the vast emptiness of space and seeing nothing but the sea of heather, hearing nothing save the occasional call of a curlew or the bleating of a sheep. Somewhere we know the crowds exist with all their noise and clamour, but for the moment we find ourselves strangely and almost frighteningly alone.

Life can bring experiences like that, experiences into which no one else seems able to enter, even into which we almost would not want anyone to enter; we just feel we could not share them. The stillness of the hills; the solitude, the loneliness that we find on the mountainside!

The mountain path speaks not only of the stillness of the hills, but of *the steepness of the way*. The smooth, the easy, the level paths and roads are found in the plains, in the valleys, but in the mountains, whether the paths pass through them or scale their peaks, they are steep and the going is hard.

If you have ever climbed Skiddaw, as I have done on two occasions to see the sun rise (and we didn't see the sun rise either time, I may say!), you will remember that first steep climb up the mountainside. In those long distant days there was an enterprising lady who used to make her way every day up to a little hut on that steepest part of the climb, carrying lemonade to be sold at a well-deserved but understandably high price to thirsty climbers. I reckon that she earned every penny of profit she made. The steepness of the way.

Yes, among the hills the path can be steep, the going hard. The temptation is to stop, to give in, to turn back, to give up. That pressure can become urgent. You will recall John Bunyan's description of Christian's ascent of the Hill Difficulty: 'I perceived that he fell from running, to going, and from going to clambering on his hands and knees

116

because of the steepness of the path.' How significant that Bunyan wrote that at the bottom of the hill there were two other ways to go, the one named Danger and the other named Destruction! There is always an alternative to the mountain paths of life, and how fierce the temptation can be to take that other way, just to give up, to give in to the difficulty because of the hardness of the going.

And what shall we say of *the sharpness of the stones*? The soft carpeting of the meadowlands and of the fields belong to the plains and the valleys that lie far below, but here, on the heights and among the hills, the paths are rough and the stones and rocks are jagged. How quickly they will cut to pieces the thin soles and the dainty footwear of the town-dweller! How deeply they will cut into the flesh of the climber when he stumbles and falls! Progress can be painful as well as slow on the mountainside. The traveller and the climber will know what it is to have cut hands and grazed knees.

Tell me, is life not like that, when wounds, and hurt, and pain, and suffering, and tears make the going almost insufferable? Yes the mountain path speaks of the sharpness of the stones. It is hard, tough going on the mountain track. But God's promise covers all that. It reads: 'I will make all my mountains a way'.

There is another thing of which our text seems to me to speak, something full of hope, full of encouragement. For we know and have experienced this, that the mountain path can become unexpectedly and surprisingly –

THE MEETING PLACE. Lonely and deserted and abandoned as the hills may at first appear, we know that others have been there before. In our Scottish Highlands we have the custom that as we move along a mountain path and come to a small cairn or pile of stones, we add our own stones to it. We know that others started to build this cairn and others will follow us, and so the path is marked out clearly.

Among those who were no strangers to the hills was the Master Himself. Again and again we find Him there. And when He makes this promise: 'I will make all my mountains a way', it is in order that the mountain path may become a meeting place with Him. How surprising some of the meetings that take place on the mountain path have been. We have suddenly noticed in the distance a tiny moving figure, so we are not alone, after all, then as the figure draws nearer suddenly we sense something familiar about it, then as it draws nearer still, suddenly our interest is stabbed awake. 'It looks like so-and-so,' we mutter to ourselves. 'It can't be, but it is, yes it is,' and with a shout we hail a friend. What if that Friend should be the Christ on the mountain path of life?

What did the mountains hold in the life of Christ. We find Him there on various occasions. In Matthew 5.1-2 we find that for Him the mountainside was *the place of instruction*: 'Seeing the multitude, Jesus went up into the mountain and when He was set, His disciples came to Him and He opened His mouth and taught them.' So the mountainside gave to them the opportunity for learning. I would submit then that there may well be some lessons that most of us are far more likely to learn on the mountain path, among the hills, than in the valleys. It may be that we shall learn more about ourselves and more about our Lord Who will meet us there.

It was also, you will recall, on a mountain that Jesus was transfigured before his disciples. Whether that mountain was Mount Tabor or Mount Hermon is a matter of debate. I, at least, will never forget the first time I visited Mount Tabor, which I am inclined to think was the more likely place. We had held, as we always did at the sacred sites in the Holy Land, a short service in the church we found at the top of the mountain. I don't know what it had meant to the rest of the party, but for me it was an unforgettable moment. As we read over quietly the story of the transfiguration, it seemed to me that a sense of that same glory filled that lovely church. Yes, the mountain slope can become for us the place of instruction, where we can learn so much more about our Lord, about ourselves.

It may well be that that lonely, steep path your feet are on right now is, in the purpose of God, going to become the

118

place where you will be led into a deeper understanding of your Lord, of yourself, or of your fellow man.

But for the Lord the mountainside was not only the place of instruction, it was also *the place of communion*: it was there that again and again we find Him at prayer. It was amid the solitude of the hills that He prayed. In Matthew 14.23 we read: 'When Jesus had sent the multitude away, He went up into a mountain and there prayed.' How often the multitudes keep us from prayer. There are multitudes of people, there are multitudes of things we have to do, until the time that should be spent in prayer becomes so short that it almost disappears from our lives. It is so often in the solitary places of life that we pray more nearly as we ought to pray.

When I go to see people in hospital, I sometimes say to them that in order to get us to look up, the good Lord has to put us on our backs! I came across a lovely saying on a card, which read: 'On earth they say, laid aside by illness; in Heaven they say, called aside for stillness'. How often in the isolation of waiting for surgery in a hospital ward, just because there is no one else to talk to or to take up our time, we talk to Him in the loneliness of that hour. At the time of some crushing anxiety, of some momentous decision, or a particular trial that is almost unbearable, or some bitter grief, we turn and share with Him our troubles, and the mountainside indeed becomes for us the place of communion too.

But for our Lord the mountain path led supremely to *the place of redemption*, for it was among the hills that He died. This has been enshrined in some of our loveliest hymns:

> There is a green hill far away,
>   Outside a city wall,
> Where the dear Lord was crucified,
>   Who died to save us all.

Or in that other old and familiar lovely song:

On a hill far away, stood an old rugged cross,
The emblem of suffering and shame

Some of us have been to the Holy City and looked up at the face of the hillside there that is called Gordon's Calvary, which many think may well have been the place where the Saviour died. It is significant to note that in Bunyan's *Pilgrim's Progress* the place where Pilgrim stumbles upon the Cross was at a place 'somewhat ascending'. Upon that place, Bunyan writes, 'stood a cross and a little below, in the bottom, a sepulchre. So I saw in my dream that just as Christian came up with the Cross, his burden loosed from off his shoulders and fell from off his back and began to tumble and so continued to do till it came to the mouth of the sepulchre where it fell in and I saw it no more.' The place where Christian lost his burden was a place 'somewhat ascending'.

Tell me, has it not so often been the case that the sinner has met the Saviour on some mountain path of difficulty, where progress has been impossible, the going hard, the pain deep, and the sense of sin and failure overwhelming. There, in the loneliness of that hour, the sinning man and the saving Lord have met 'at a place somewhat ascending', and the burden of sin has loosed from off our backs and fallen tumbling, until it, too, has come to the mouth of the sepulchre where it has fallen in and we, too, praise be to God, have seen it no more! Our text then has spoken to us of the mountain path, of the meeting place, and yet again of –

THE MASTER'S PLAN. Listen exactly to what the promise says in our text: 'I will make all my mountains *a way*.' Paths are meant to lead somewhere – either they lead through the mountains or up the mountains – and the Master's plan is that the mountain path is going to lead somewhere in your spiritual experience and in mine.

This suggests that this mountain path will prove to be a *way that is productive*. It will lead me somewhere. It may lead to a closer walk with Him, it may lead to a deeper and simpler faith in Him, it may lead to a truer likeness to Him. When the Lord planned the path, when He tells me that He will make all my mountains a way, He is not wasting His time, surely, nor is He wasting your time or mine. The mountain path speaks to me of a way that is productive.

But our text also contains a *word that is inclusive*. It is the little word 'all'. 'I will make *all* my mountains a way.' Some of the mountain paths, we are prepared to believe, will lead us somewhere, but we find it difficult to believe that 'all' mountain paths lead somewhere. But the promise of God stands and we do well to rest our hearts and minds upon the word that is inclusive. There is another verse from the New Testament which says: 'All things work together for good to them that love God.' Dear old Bishop Taylor Smith used to comment on that, 'not ninety-nine things out of a hundred, but ninety-nine things and one.' 'All things', 'all my mountains'. How we delight to make exceptions where God makes none. We say, 'All?, yes, all, but not this. . .' But God's word does say, 'I will make *all* my mountains a way.'

I want to suggest to you that this calls for *a will that is submissive*. For me and for you, this is the way, and there is no other. I suppose that one of the best-known Christians who knew more about suffering than most of us have ever known or are ever likely to know was that lovely lady Amy Wilson Carmichael, who went to India to work among the temple children. If you can get hold of her books then grab them with both hands, particularly if you are travelling the mountains. She knew all about them. The theme occurs again and again. Listen to these lines:

> God of the Heights, austere, inspiring,
> Thy word hath come to me.
> O let no selfish aims, conspiring,
> Distract my soul from Thee.
> Loosen me from Things of Time,
> Strengthen me for steadfast climb.

121

The Temporal would bind my spirit,
Father, be Thou my Stay.
Show me that flesh cannot inherit,
Stored for another day.
Be transparent, Things of Time;
Looking through you, I would climb.

Now by Thy grace my spirit chooseth
Treasure that shall abide.
The great Unseen, I know, endureth,
My footsteps shall not slide.
Not for me the Things of Time;
God of mountains, I will climb.

Here is another of her poems:

Make us Thy mountaineers;
We would not linger on the lower slope,
Fill us afresh with hope, O God of Hope,
That undefeated we may climb the hill
As seeing Him who is invisible.

Let us die climbing. When this little while
Lies far behind us, and the last defile
Is all alight, and in that light we see
Our Leader and our Lord, what will it be?

And then this final one:

Make me to be Thy happy mountaineer,
O God most high;
My climbing soul would welcome the austere:
Lord, crucify
On rock or scree, ice-cliff or field of snow,
The softness that would sink to things below.

Thou art my Guide; where Thy sure feet have trod
Shall mine be set;
Thy lightest word my law of life, O God,
Lest I forget,

And slip and fall, teach me to do Thy will,
Thy mountaineer upon Thy holy hill.

So our text stands – what a promise, what a prospect. The mountain path becomes the meeting place, and then unfolds the Master's plan. On the mountain path, among the hills, we are never alone, and need never be afraid.

14

JEREMIAH: IN THE HANDS OF THE POTTER

'Behold, as the clay is in the potter's hand, so are ye in mine hand' (Jeremiah 18.6).

I remember reading somewhere that a great preacher of a former generation had said that what people needed most was comfort, and I am quite sure that every Christian will agree that oftentimes it has been for comfort and encouragement that our souls have cried out. So often our experience has been disappointing and we have become disheartened in our Christian life. May I then bring to you one of the rarest and truest words of comfort from the pages of the old Book, with the prayer so that what has been a great cheer to my own soul, may be an encouraging word to you.

We shall find this word in that familiar passage in Jeremiah 18, where we read of the vessel marred in the hand of the potter and then made again into another vessel. For a long time I had thought of this passage solely as having a message for the unconverted man or woman, and from it I had preached the gospel of God's grace to the unbelieving sinner. Of course that was all quite proper and true, that the life which has been marred by sin could be made again, a new creation in Christ Jesus.

But the lives of the unbelievers are not the only lives marred by sin, and I well remember the new light which came upon this passage when I realised one day that the spiritual application of this incident was not so much to the unbelieving sinner as to the sinning believer, to the life which had known, like Israel, deliverance upon deliverance, privilege upon privilege, and yet, in spite of all that God had done, had still fallen away from His will!

Let us recall first of all the exact words of Scripture: 'I went down to the potter's house, and, behold, he wrought a work on the wheels. And the vessel that he made of clay was marred in the hand of the potter: so he made it again another vessel . . . then the word of the Lord came unto me saying, as clay is in the hands of the potter, so are ye in Mine hand.'

Some years ago I had the opportunity of going over the great Wedgwood Pottery works, and amongst the many things I saw that day was a potter at work moulding the clay with his hands. I shall never forget seeing that shapeless mass of clay grow into a thing of beauty under the hands of the potter, and what I saw then has helped me in some measure to understand the spiritual meaning behind these words of Scripture. The first thought that I would bring to you is this, that here we are reminded of –

THE PRESSURE OF THE HANDS OF GOD. 'As the clay is in the hands of the potter, so are ye in mine hand.' When I stood watching the potter at work, it was his hands that held my attention, and wonderful it was to see that clay taking on form and symmetry under the pressure of the potter's hands. 'The pressure of the hands of God' – what a wonderful thought that is, that the hands of God are seeking day by day to mould these shapeless lives of ours into things of beauty!

I wonder if you can remember the day on which you committed that life of yours into the hands of God, at the moment of your conversion! How do the words of the chorus put it?

> Into the hands that were wounded to save me
> Into the hands that are mighty to keep,
> Into the hands that can guide me and guard me,
> Saviour, my life I yield.

Do you remember the day, the very place it may have been? Since that moment the wheel of time has been turning swiftly and your life, and mine, has known the 'pressure of the hands of God'.

We might well ask how it is that our lives know the pressure of the hands of God. The Scriptures speak of at least two ways in which this happens and I think that our testimony confirms the teaching of the Word.

Firstly, I would suggest inwardly, *through conviction*. Do you remember the words of the psalmist in Psalm 32.4? 'Day and night Thy hand was heavy upon me,' and the context would seem to imply that the experience was one of an inward conviction of soul, that conviction which is the work of the Holy Spirit.

Tell me, have you not known such an experience? It may have started in some meeting or convention in the quiet of your own room, or in a service in church, but day and night after that you have not been able to get away from the conviction that has come into your soul. It may have been about something wrong in your life, or about something that you felt that God wanted you to do or be. For you, too, it has been true that day and night the hands of God have been heavy upon you! Yes, I am sure that every Christian has known something of that pressure.

The second way in which we feel the pressure of the hands of God is not inwardly through conviction, but outwardly, *through circumstances*. Again, the psalmist helps us, when in Psalm 31.15 he says, 'My times are in Thy hands.' Has it not been so? How wonderfully circumstances have moulded our lives, very often circumstances over which we ourselves have no control.

I think of the Christian home. What some of us owe to the fact that we were brought up in a Christian home only eternity will reveal! The influence of Godly parents, their prayers and example – what an impression they have made on our lives! I think again of the influence of a spiritual ministry. How great the privilege enjoyed by so many, of worshipping in a church where the Word of God is proclaimed in its fullness and in the power of the Holy Spirit, and how much we owe to such a circumstance in our life!

I think yet again of the hardship of changed circumstances, the strange new life in the Services to which in times of war so many of our young people have been called, and how their lives bear the impress of these! What shall we say of the trials of sickness, of sorrow? How many and many a life has been wonderfully changed through such circumstances! Was it not an invalid herself, Frances Ridley Havergal, who wrote, 'When the pressure is sorest the hands must be nearest'? 'The pressure of the hands of God' – yes, all our lives have known it, inwardly through conviction, and outwardly through circumstances.

The second thought I give you from the verses in the old Book is this, that we are reminded here of –

THE PURPOSE IN THE MIND OF GOD. 'Behold he wrought a work on the wheels.' As I watched the hands of the potter at work, I gradually found that my attention was being transferred from the hands of the potter to the clay itself. As I watched him at work I suddenly realised that in the clay was being revealed the pattern which was in his mind. Gradually it became clear, until at last in its finished perfection it stood complete! I wonder how far your lives and mine are revealing to the watching world the purpose and pattern which are in the mind of God for us! As I watched the clay I could see that design taking shape. Can the watching world see the purpose which is in the mind of God taking shape before their eyes in our daily walk and conversation?

'The purpose in the Mind of God' – I wonder what that purpose is? Again the potter may be able to help us here, for I think it would be true to say that one of two motives govern his mind. Either he creates something for its usefulness or for its beauty. When we think of the Divine purpose, does that not also follow these two main lines; usefulness and that beauty which the Scriptures call holiness? I wonder how far this twofold purpose of the Divine Potter is being revealed in your life and mine?

Loveliness. Again and again the Bible speaks of 'The beauty of holiness'. This is most certainly part of the purpose in the mind of God for us, for we read that 'He will beautify the meek with salvation' (Psalm 149.4), and that part of that purpose is 'that we might be partakers of His holiness' (Hebrews 12.10), and again in 1 Thessalonians 4.3: 'This is the will of God, even your sanctification.' Surely it is part of that purpose that your life and mine might show forth something of the loveliness and strength of Jesus Christ. I wonder how far the clay of our humanity is revealing the wonder of the Divine pattern. So many Christian lives are so utterly unlovely. Well might Gypsy Smith, the evangelist, sing, 'Can others see Jesus in you?' How does that verse go?

> To dwell above with the saints we love
>   That will be bliss and glory!
> But to dwell below with the saints we know
>   Is quite a different story!

Usefulness. It is certainly part of the intention of God for the soul of the believer that he should be useful for service! In John 15.16 we have the words of Christ, 'Ye have not chosen Me, but I have chosen you, and ordained you, that ye should go and bring forth fruit, and that your fruit should remain.' Some of you may remember the story told of Bishop Taylor Smith when he was dining with a friend on one occasion and they had reached the stage when the fruit was being served. The bishop had taken up a fruit knife, one of those silver knives with mother-of-pearl handles, pretty to look at but usually rather blunt, and he was faced with some difficulty when he attempted to cut the fruit he had chosen. Thereupon he turned to his friend and said with that twinkle of his, 'This knife is like many Christians, stainless but quite useless!'

It is, alas, only too true that the pattern in the mind of God, as far as usefulness is concerned in so many of our lives, seems to be frustrated by our own wilfulness. Yet it is so clearly fulfilled in so many other lives. I am quite certain that many of us have come across Christian people who seem to shed the fragrance of Christ around them wherever they go. Whenever we meet them we are strengthened and blessed. They may be the most ordinary people to look at, but extraordinary in the influence they exert for God.

The pressure of the hands of God. The purpose in the mind of God. The third and most wonderful thought that we are here reminded of is –

THE PATIENCE OF THE LOVE OF GOD. 'Marred in the hands of the potter, so He made it again another vessel.' 'Marred'! Would that word not need to be written across every Christian life; across your life and mine! How wonderful then is this gem of spiritual truth for such as ourselves, that for the marred vessel there is the comfort of the patience of the love of God. Yes, there may be *a tragedy to be faced in the lives of men*. Yes, something had gone wrong (how often and how easily things do go wrong in the realm of the spirit!). Was there some fault in the clay? It may have been too soft or too dry in one place and so for the time being the purpose of the potter has been thwarted until he has dealt with the fault. The addition of some more sand or moisture, as the case may be, has been required. But I note this, that the steadfastness of His purpose never falters: 'Marred, so he made it again'. There is here no word of recrimination, no impatient rejection of the clay, which speaks to me of *a constancy to be found in the love of God*.

What a picture of God's dealings with us! Have not His purposes for us, and through us for others, been thwarted again and again by something faulty and sinful in our lives? There has been something with which God has had to deal before being able to continue His gracious work in us! It has been a time when the beauty of holiness that was beginning to be revealed has been sadly marred, a time when our incipent usefulness to God has been destroyed. But, blessed be God, although we have been, and it may be still are, marred vessels, we are still in the hands of the potter.

It may well be a costly and a painful experience while God deals with us! See the potter's hands breaking down the half-formed vessel so that he might remedy the defect!

We, too, may know something of that breaking down, before God can once again go on with His gracious ministry in us and through us.

Is there some 'marred vessel' reading these lines today? You have known, thank God, the pressure of the hands of God in the past. More than that, your life has also shown signs of the purpose of the mind of God. But today finds you a 'marred vessel', though still in the Hands of the Potter. May I give you one word in closing? The word is just this: I read in the Word of God of something else that was 'marred'. We have been thinking of the marred vessel; do you remember the 'marred visage' (Isaiah 52.14)? Will you look up into that 'marred visage' now, and tell me what you can see there? If you feel you dare not, may I tell you what I have seen there for myself? I see there perfect forgiveness, unchanging love, and an unfaltering purpose. Lay hold afresh today of Christ and realise the wonder of the patience of the eternal love of God. Will you again rest back upon that forgiveness and that love, and although you are today a 'marred vessel', yet in simple trust yield yourself to His hands that He may make you from today – 'another vessel'.

15

JEREMIAH: THE UNEXPECTED PLACE OF BLESSING

'Grace in the wilderness' (Jeremiah 31.2).

'The people found grace in the wilderness.' I remember well how these words in Jeremiah 31.2 challenged me many years ago when I first stumbled on them. Recently they have challenged me afresh. The text speaks to me of –

A PLACE THAT WAS DESOLATE. The people were in the wilderness; and life as we know it has at times a great deal in common with the wilderness. The wilderness speaks to me of *dreariness* – the same unvarying, unchanging monotony of desolation. One of the vivid memories of a flight to Kenya is of the vast expanse of desert wastes above which our plane flew for so long. Has not life something in common with this, sometimes? Have you known life to possess an unchanging, unattractive monotony that has made you think it scarcely worth living? And although you have looked in every direction, you have seen no possibility of change. A place that is desolate!

But this dreariness is due in the main to the fact that the wilderness is also a place of *death*. So little that is living is to be found there. Have you known what it is to see something die which has been precious to you beyond words? What a wilderness life is if love has died; and how many homes there are today where love has died, love between husband and wife. Show me a home like that and I will show you a world that has become a wilderness; a world that once was full of fragrant hopes and fair and lovely promise, but is now a desolation and a ruin. What a wilderness life is if faith has died: the faith of friend in friend, or of parent in child, or child in parent; to discover in one terrible moment that the one we trusted utterly is unworthy of our trust. What a wilderness life is if hope has died, if our dreams fade finally and for ever before our very eyes. Have you known what it is to live on through the most severe trial, sustained only by the hopes, the dreams of what might be, of what you pray desperately will be? And then one day you are stunned by the discovery, in the cold light of facts you cannot ignore, that your dream has vanished, your hopes are dead, and in a moment your whole world has turned grey.

But the wilderness is not only a place of dreariness and of death, it is also a place of *danger*. The fact that it is a place of death spells danger to the living who enter it, who have to pass that way. Every caravan trail through the great deserts of the world has been marked by the whitened bones of men and beasts who have perished ere they could emerge from the desert. And the supreme peril that threatens the souls of men when they enter upon the wilderness experiences of life is not so much that so many of the lovely and precious things in life are found to have died there, but that life itself is imperilled, and they themselves should perish in the desolate wastes. Many a life of usefulness to God has been lost in some wilderness of life, and nothing today remains save the whitened bones, the few traces and memories of a life that has been lived, but is lost. A place that is desolate – is it any wonder then that the words of our text speak also of –

A PATH THAT WAS DREADED. No one ever took the way through the wilderness unless he had to, and no one who faced it did so in any spirit of happiness or enjoyment. The path would test every fibre in a man's courage, it would demand every atom of physical endurance; survival of life itself would be constantly in the balance. Is it any wonder that the wilderness was a dreaded place, and the path through it shunned and avoided, taken only out of sheer necessity?

What are the elements that make the wilderness paths of life, dreaded paths. I think first of *The loneliness of the way*. You don't find many others in the wilderness. For days, for weeks it may be, you will journey on and on and never meet another soul. What loneliness is there to compare to life without love? To live on without anyone to care about us, to feel with us in our sorrows, to rejoice with us in our joys and triumphs, to share our burdens and anxieties, to quieten our fears. Since the day we knew the tenderness of a mother's love, every heart craves at times to be loved. But it may be that we are growing old, and almost all of our loved ones have gone, there may even be no one left to care, and the way of life in our old age has become very lonely. Or our loneliness may be due to the fact that we are the only Christians in the family, or it may just be that love has died where once it lived, and loneliness instead of love is our portion, and the path through the wilderness has become a dreaded path.

But it may be that the path is dreaded because of *the hardness of the way*. The track through the wilderness is no easy road. It may mean oppressive heat by day, and at times biting cold at night; it speaks of parched lips and burning thirst, blistered feet and aching limbs, it means a constant battle against weariness, the body crying out for respite, the mind knowing that to give in would be to perish. What way in life so hard as that where hope has died, when our dreams have vanished and gone? Parents have lived for a child, facing deprivation and sacrifice for themselves so as to give all they could to the one they loved. They have dreamed their dreams as to what their child would be and do; and then, one day, their dreams were broken, their hopes shattered, when death took the little one out of their arms and gave it to God. Or it may have been some dream that kept a man going through all the hardness of life's way, some dream of future love and happiness. He loved a girl and had the promise of her love in return, and around that mutual love he built his life; and when a time of separation came, wherever he went he carried her picture in his heart and her name on his lips; and in the darkest hour the brightness of his dreams and hopes gave him courage to go on, until the letter came that told him that his dreams were only dreams. Surely it is one of the hardest things in life to go on when hopes have died and dreams have faded, when the thing that gave courage to go on is gone, when the longing and hope that were almost life itself suddenly wither and die. Yes, the hardness of the way makes the wilderness a dreaded path.

But the path is also dreaded because of *the emptiness of the way*. There is so little in the wilderness. Dust, sand, rocks, stones, heat – but there is no sound of running water, no whisper of the wind in the trees, no singing of the birds, no fragrance of, no beauty of flowers, no refreshing shade and green grass. Nothing, but emptiness and silence. Does life not know something of this emptiness when faith has died? Faith in another is the source of so much that enriches life, but to lose faith is to lose all. When the spring dries up it is not long before the ground it watered becomes arid and barren, dead and empty!

If our text had no more than this to say, it would be a sorry picture to draw; but I read here of –

A PLAN THAT WAS DISCOVERED. 'The people *found grace* in the wilderness.' In that place which was desolate, on that path which was dreaded, in the most unlikely place, they made the most unexpected discovery. God's people have found three things which for them made the wilderness blossom as the rose.

The three things which I find in God's word to be associated with the wilderness are firstly, *a daily provision*. Christ reminded His hearers on one occasion that 'your fathers did eat manna *in the wilderness*'. The manna was given daily, and had to be gathered daily. It was gathered early in the morning, or else not at all, for when the sun waxed hot it melted away. We are told that 'the children of Israel did eat manna forty years until. . .' they left the wilderness. They had never seen it before, they never saw it afterwards; but while they were in the wilderness they never lacked the sustenance they needed. We need to learn this lesson, that God's grace is always commensurate with man's need. But I must take what God offers, and take it daily, or die.

The second thing I note concerning the wilderness is *the Divine presence*. In Exodus 13.18, 21 we read that the Lord 'led the people about, through *the way of the wilderness* . . . and the Lord went before them by day in a pillar of cloud, to lead them in the way; and by night in a pillar of fire, to give them light'. I said earlier that the path through the wilderness was dreaded because of its emptiness and loneliness, but the one great fact which challenges the stumbling soul is that although life may be emptied of human love, although the dreams and hopes that have buoyed us up and given us courage have vanished, although even faith is broken, yet God remains. We are not alone. Life is not empty as long as God is in it. 'He took not away the pillar from before the people.' The traveller throughout the wilderness is not unaccompanied. We are not forsaken. We are not desolate. Nothing can separate us from the love of God, and nothing can pluck us out of His hands. It is sometimes only 'in the wilderness' that we discover the reality of His presence and the sweetness of communion with Him.

The last thing that I want to note with you as being associated with the wilderness is *the definite purpose*. In the book of Acts I read of a man in the midst of a thriving and happy ministry; but 'the angel of the Lord spake unto Philip, saying, Arise, and go toward the south . . . unto Gaza, *which is desert* . . . and he arose and went: and, behold, a man. . .' I cannot believe that it was easy for Philip to go; but I can at least learn this, that there was a clearly defined purpose in the move, a purpose and plan that held something far beyond Philip's knowledge or understanding. Philip was busy winning a town for Christ; God wanted him to influence a whole nation through one man God wanted him to meet in the wilderness! Although it meant leaving the warmth of fellowship in Samaria, and the thrill and wonder of witnessing God's power, for the loneliness of the wilderness way, the day was to come when Philip would thank God for that wilderness experience, just as you and I will do one day, if we are as watchful and as obedient to the purpose of God in the wilderness. We may not understand, but it may well be that God is taking us to the wilderness just because there is someone else there that must be won, and He wants us to be the instrument in the winning of that one; and God alone knows what issues may depend upon the winning of that one to faith in Christ.

What God's purpose is for you and for me in the wilderness I cannot begin to say; but this I do know, there is a purpose which, if hidden to us at the moment, is clear to the mind of God, and for which one day we shall thank God as we find ourselves in the number of the people who 'found grace in the wilderness'.

16

DANIEL: THE HIDDEN SECRETS OF TRUE GREATNESS

'A man greatly beloved' (Daniel 10.11).

Somewhere or other in my reading I came across a phrase which has remained vividly in my mind. It runs, 'For every tree growing up there is a tree growing down.' In no life is this principle more vividly illustrated than in the life of Daniel. For too many of us, Daniel is simply a man who was delivered from the lions. He was, of course, a great man, but behind his outward greatness there was a hidden life of communion and fellowship with his God.

The words of our text in which Daniel is named, 'a man greatly beloved', are words spoken not on earth, but in heaven: though I am sure that what was said in heaven was but an echo of what so many said of him on earth. He was to so many 'a man greatly beloved'. When reading through the book of Daniel these words seemed to me to leap out of the page and it came home to me with great force how true it is that from time to time, and, alas, only too rarely, one comes across lives of which these words can be said. I found myself thinking how well we could do with many more such men and then I found myself asking what was the secret behind such a life? What were and are the conditioning factors that make such a life possible? Are there any clues to be found in the life of Daniel – clues which will have a corresponding place in any other life so described? When reading through this tenth chapter of Daniel, I came across these two verses, 10 and 11, and it seemed that here we could find the answer.

I want us to note that Daniel was a man whom we find –

ON HIS FACE BEFORE GOD. Verse 9: 'Then I was on my face.' He was a man who suffered no illusions about himself. He knew what he was in the sight of God. Robert Murray McCheyne, the saintly young Scottish Presbyterian minister, wrote, 'What a minister is on his knees in secret before God Almighty – that he is and no more.' What Robert Murray McCheyne wrote about a minister he could just as well have written about any Christian. What a Christian is on his knees in secret before God Almighty – that he is and no more! How those words cut all of us down to size!

It was the realisation of what he was that brought Daniel down on his face before his God. I want us to note *the vision that forced him there*. The vision was one of glory and splendour. It is recorded in vv.5 and 6. The description reminds us vividly of the vision of the Lord of Glory recorded in the book of Revelation, Chapter 1, where, as a result of that vision, John states, 'And when I saw Him, I fell at His Feet as one dead.' It reminds us, too, of the vision that came to Isaiah recorded in Isaiah Chapter 6. You remember when Isaiah saw the Lord high and lifted up, he cried out, 'Woe is me, for I am undone. I am a man unclean.' When Joshua faced the Divine Captain before Jericho, he, too, fell on his face before him. When Simon Peter realised something of the wonder and the power of His Master, he, too, fell down before him. It is significant, is it not, that when St. Paul describes the universality of sin he speaks of it against the background of, 'the Glory of God'. In Romans 3.23, he writes, 'All have sinned and come short of the Glory of God.'

The point that emerges is simply this, that at the heart of any such life is an awareness of the splendour and the glory, the righteousness and the majesty of God Himself. And it is strange, but true, that a deep consciousness of sin does not arise so much from an experience of sin as from a vision of the righteousness and holiness of God.

We will not pause to debate who it was that Daniel saw. Some scholars say it was the Lord Himself. Others say that it was one of the archangels. Whichever interpretation be true, the vision was one of glory such as did not belong to earth, but to heaven. So it is that in 2 Corinthians 4.6 Paul describes the significance of the coming of Jesus Christ in similar terms. 'God who commanded the light to shine out of darkness hath shined in our hearts to give the light of the knowledge of the glory of God in the face of Jesus Christ.' There we note the vision that forced him there.

And leading on from that, we note *the verdict that faced him there*. It was a verdict concerning himself. Daniel 10.8: 'Therefore I was left alone and saw this great vision and there remained no strength in me for my comeliness was turned in me into corruption.' Here was a verdict concerning himself. And that verdict was reached when he found himself alone. Most of us are pretty good at passing verdicts upon others, but when Daniel found himself alone at that hour, the verdict that he faced was one that he had to pass upon himself.

More and more I am learning that at the heart of all true spiritual living is an essential loneliness. It seems inescapable. It seems that God wants to deal with us, to meet with us alone. Fellowship with other Christians is a wonderful thing. Indeed, it is one of the most wonderful things about the Christian life, but the basic thing about the Christian experience is not so much fellowship with other Christians as fellowship with God. And, for that, we have to find ourselves alone. Do you remember that it was when Jacob was 'left alone' that there came a man and wrestled with him until the breaking of the day?

What, then, was the verdict that Daniel faced when he found himself alone? It was a verdict covering two aspects of his life. The first was that he had a deep sense of his own helplessness. He says, 'I retained no strength.' How the Old Testament here harmonises with the New. Do you remember the words of our Lord to His disciples concerning their spiritual effectiveness, words recorded in John 15.5, where He said to them, 'Without me, ye can do nothing'? These words remind us of the other prophetic statement in Zechariah 4.6, where we find the following recorded: 'Not by might nor by power, but by my Spirit, says the Lord of Hosts.'

The first verdict then, was one concerning his own helplessness. The second concerned a sense of his own sinfulness. Daniel states, 'My comeliness was turned in me into corruption.' It is a strange paradox, but true to experience, that the greatest saints in the eyes of men consider themselves to be the greatest sinners in the sight of God. Sister Eva of Friedenshort did wonderful work amongst children in Germany and yet we find her saying about herself, 'I saw in myself nothing but sin, incapability and weakness.' This, of course, was the verdict that St. Paul recorded about himself when he wrote, 'I know that in me, that is to say, in my flesh, (my nature apart from the grace of God) there dwelleth no good thing.' It is significant then, is it not, that a sense of sin is based not upon an experience of sin, but upon a knowledge of righteousness? I remember very clearly in my younger days when I was a scoutmaster, one of the patrol leaders, a butcher's apprentice, speaking at the scouts' own Bible class, making this comment. He said to his brother scouts, 'You know that when your Mum hangs out the washing it looks white . . . until,' he added, 'the snow falls.' How true that when the best of human whiteness is matched against the spotless dazzling perfection of God's holiness, even man's white turns grey.

So we find the first part of the secret of Daniel's life – we find him on his face before God.

The second thing I see here is that Daniel is a man we find –

ON HIS KNEES BEFORE GOD. Verse 10: 'And behold a hand touched me which set me upon my knees and upon the palms of my hands.'

I suppose that one of the better known verses in the book of Daniel is that found in Daniel 6.9 and 10, when his enemies tricked King Darius into making a decree that they knew would implicate Daniel and bring about his downfall and death in the lion's den. The decree demanded that nobody was to bow in worship before any other god than

King Darius himself. And we read, 'Now when Daniel knew that the writing was signed, he went into his house, and his windows being open in his chamber towards Jerusalem, he kneeled upon his knees, three times a day and prayed and gave thanks before his God as he did aforetime.' How true that remark I have already quoted, that 'for every tree growing up there is a tree growing down'. And that behind the life that men see there is the life that God sees.

Think of *the intimacy that this man enjoyed*. As I pointed out earlier, the description of Daniel as a man greatly beloved applied to heaven, albeit the echo would, no doubt, be heard on earth. There are those men whose ambitions are that they should find themselves in the so-called corridors of power on earth whether in the political world, the industrial world, or even, alas, in the ecclesiastical world. And, on a smaller scale maybe, in the parochial world. But the real corridors of power are in the spiritual world.

Do you recall how Paul describes the Christians in a series of paradoxical statements in 2 Corinthians 6.9 ff? Amongst other paradoxes he begins by saying that the Christians are 'unknown and yet well-known'. They are, apparently, unknown comparatively on earth and yet well known in heaven! Paul goes on with a whole string of paradoxes. He continues, 'As dying and behold, we live. As chastened, and not killed. As sorrowful, yet always rejoicing. As poor, yet making many rich. As having nothing, yet possessing all things.'

In presenting his report to the Presbytery of Dundee on the revival in his church, St. Peter's, Robert Murray McCheyne had this to say about the men who were so greatly used by God at that time. He reports, 'They are, in general, I believe, peculiarly given to secret prayer.' In Daniel, we find a man who enjoyed a deep intimacy with his Lord. If there are few men of power today, is it because there are few men of prayer?

We note, also, *the fidelity this man displayed*. Nothing was allowed to break the disciplined pattern of prayer that

141

he had formed. His custom was to pray three times a day and when he knew of the plot of his enemies, that knowledge did nothing to interrupt his habit. I was interested in my reading to discover that both John Wesley and the great Methodist preacher, the late Dr. W. E. Sangster of London, had made the same resolve that they would give the first hour of each day to God.

No wonder Daniel's influence was so great. Verse 12 records the fact that his prayers were heard and that at once the wheels of God's mercy began to turn. We have no time to go into the area of spiritual conflict of which we get a brief glimpse in this verse. We cannot but remind ourselves, as Paul does, that 'the weapons of our warfare are not carnal, but mighty through God to the pulling down of strongholds' (2 Corinthians 10.4). And again, in Ephesians 6.12, Paul writes, 'We wrestle not against flesh and blood but against principalities, against powers, against spiritual wickedness in high places.' What John Bunyan calls 'the weapon of all prayer' is decisive in this area of conflict. And Daniel, 'The Man Greatly Beloved', not only knew the truth about himself and was found on his face before God, but he knew the truth about his God and was found on his knees before God. The intimacy this man enjoyed and the fidelity this man displayed.

There is one more clue that gives us some insight as to the secret of this man's life, for we find him also in these verses –

ON HIS FEET BEFORE GOD. In verse 11, the word came, 'Stand up. Stand upright, and Daniel stood trembling.' That was where he stood on his feet before God. I am reminded of the words of Elijah to Ahab, 'As the Lord God of Israel liveth before whom I stand.' That was where the servant stood. Do you recall the words of the Queen of Sheba to King Solomon in 1 Kings 10.8, 'Happy are these they servants which stand continually before thee.' Standing before God suggests two things. The first is *the availability of the servant*. The servant was there to do his Master's bidding, to do anything his Master required, whether great or small. At the great Keswick Convention in England one year, when I was one of the speakers on the Thursday evening when, traditionally, we consider the enabling ministry of the Holy Spirit, I felt led to speak on the Character of Stephen. Three times a word is used to describe him – the word 'full', in Acts, Chapters 6 and 7. Although we don't find the word fulness in the New Testament, we do find either the verb 'filled', or the adjective 'full', used frequently, so, obviously, the word 'fullness' is not entirely out of place. I remember summing up the ministry of the Holy Spirit in the life of Stephen in relation to this word used again and again to describe him – 'full'. I spoke of how fullness *serves*, how fullness *speaks*, how fullness *shines*.

It was the first of these aspects of the life of Stephen that gripped me, how fullness serves! For the first thing we find Stephen doing is counting the collection and looking after the widows. He was prepared to do anything, small or great. And Daniel was like that. His greatness and his great career all started in a small way when we are told that he refused to eat the food set before him. This food had, no doubt, been offered to idols, and to him, as a Jew, the food therefore was unclean. Great things followed later, for the story of Daniel illustrates what our Lord spoke about in the Parable of the Talents in Matthew 25 when He talked of the servants who had been faithful. Do you remember what he said? 'Thou hast been faithful over a few things; I will make thee ruler over many things.' Faithfulness in the small things leads to the opportunity of proving ourselves faithful in the big things! And so we note the availability of the Servant. Some servants of God, so-called, are only available for the big occasions, for the big opportunities. The true servant of God is available for anything, small or great.

Leading on, though, from the consideration of the availability of the servant, we face in the second place *the accountability of the servant*. Daniel records of that moment, 'I stood trembling'. His words remind me of Paul's counsel in Philippians 2.12, where he said to the Christians

143

at Philippi, 'Work out your own salvation with fear and trembling.' Is this the fear of a tyrant? Most certainly, not! It is the fear of disappointing one we love. I remember hearing about a young boy at school who was being pressurised by some of his companions to do something that he knew to be wrong. He stood his ground. But they went on taunting him and teasing him and finally one said to this boy, 'Are you afraid your Dad will hurt you if he finds out what you have done?' To which the boy replied, 'No, I am not afraid my Dad would hurt me, but I am afraid I would hurt my Dad.' Surely it is the fear of love, the fear of disappointing One whom we love and respect and long to please. We are reminded again and again in the New Testament that there is to be a judgment of believers, not a judgment concerning our sin – that judgment took place on the Cross – but a judgment concerning our service. In Romans 14.12, Paul writes that, 'Everyone of us shall give account of himself to God.' Again, in 1 Corinthians 4.3-4, we find Paul speaking of the fact that 'He that judgeth me is the Lord.' A Christian lives under the constant judgment of love. And because the only judgment that really matters is the judgment of his God, the Christian is able to say, like St. Paul, 'I count it a very small thing that I should be judged of you, or of man's judgment.' This was what was said of John Knox, was it not, that 'he feared the face of no man because he feared the face of God.' This was the one quality which John Wesley longed to find and you may remember that he said, 'Give me one hundred preachers who fear nothing but sin and desire nothing but God, and I care not a straw whether they be clergymen or laymen – such alone will shake the gates of hell and set up the Kingdom of God on earth.'

So we find Daniel standing on his feet before God, albeit tremblingly, so that he may then stand on his feet before men and do that fearlessly. Is it any wonder that in heaven he was thus named as 'A Man Greatly Beloved'.

17

HOSEA: THE DISCIPLINE OF WITHDRAWAL

'Ephraim is joined to idols, let him alone' (Hosea 4.17).

I am sure that all of us have had the experience of hearing a phrase that has stuck in our minds and memories and has proved unforgettable. Many years ago when I was vicar of St. James's Church, Carlisle, and in my first charge, I invited the late Mr. R. Hudson Pope of the then C.S.S.M. to come and take a mission for me. It had been under his ministry in my prep-school days that I had come to a clear understanding of what it meant to be a Christian. He had gladly come. It was at one of the smaller meetings, when he was speaking to the large Youth Fellowship, that this, to me unforgetable, phrase came from his lips. He was commenting on the verse which we have taken as our text, and the comment was this: 'What we will not learn by precept we must then learn by experience.'

I want us to think through the meaning of this and to take as our theme what I have called 'the discipline of withdrawal'. In the first instance I want us to note that here we have –

A DISOBEDIENCE THAT WAS BLATANT. 'Ephraim is joined to idols.' We are concerned in this study with two things, first, *what God had revealed*. God's will in this matter had been made perfectly plain in the second commandment, 'Thou shalt not make unto thyself any graven image.' There were, no doubt, very good reasons behind this prohibition. In this area there lay two very real dangers, the first being that of dishonouring their God, and the second that of endangering their own highest good. The idolatry of the tribes that surrounded God's chosen people was saturated with immorality. God's glory and Israel's good were both involved.

Both of these matters, God's glory and man's good, are also the concern of God in the fuller revelation of Himself and His will in the New Testament. Here, too, we find a God Who has revealed Himself, and in our obedience to the truth revealed in and through the person of Jesus Christ lies the way to that fullness of Life that God in His mercy and love has planned for man. 'I am come,' said Jesus Christ, 'that they might have life and that they might have it more abundantly.' This message of the discipline of withdrawal is, then, for those who have heard the truth, and who therefore know perfectly well what they are doing! No plea of ignorance was valid for Ephraim, nor is it valid for ourselves now. We too are concerned with the revealed will of God, with truth that we have come to know.

We note also *how man had rebelled.* The issue was over a matter of flagrant and deliberate disobedience, a defiance of and a disregard for God's revealed will. 'Ephraim is joined to idols.' It will help us to understand the undertones of this message when we realise that the whole background to this prophecy was the broken home and broken heart of the prophet Hosea himself. He was a man whose wife had proved unfaithful to her marriage vows, and was now openly living the life of a prostitute. There was apparently no sense of shame, no hint of repentance. Here then was a sin, a disobedience that was as blatant as hers, in the life of the nation. The whole background was one of spiritual infidelity on the part of Israel to her God.

The New Testament counterpart to all this is found in the opening chapter of Paul's great letter to the Romans. There in Chapter 1, verse 21, we read of Paul's condemnation of man in these words: 'When they knew God, they glorified Him not as God.' God's word in our text is directed to those who know what they are doing and who know that they are disobeying the revealed truth and will of God. In my travels around the world I often feel that this is the basic problem that God has with His people. It is not that we need to learn and discover anything new, but rather that we need to stop disobeying God in those matters of which we are fully informed and aware. We begin, then, with the fact of a disobedience that was blatant.

But let us complete the words of our text, 'Ephraim is joined to idols, *let him alone.*' Scholars differ as to what these final words mean and they find two possible interpretations. I don't think that we need to be committed to one or the other; it may well be that we are justified in taking both together. In experience certainly both apply. The first interpretation suggests that God was Himself going to leave Ephraim alone, the other suggests that Judah was being told to have no dealings with Ephraim. Whichever way we interpret the words, they speak to us of the second point we need to make, and that is that here we are thinking of –

A DISCIPLINE THAT WAS BITTER. Let us pause for a moment and recall that memorable phrase of Hudson Pope, 'What we will not learn by precept we must then learn by experience.' If we turn back again to that first chapter in Paul's letter to the Romans, we find that this same principle is in operation. In verse 24 we read that 'God gave them up . . .' to what they had chosen. In Proverbs 1.29 we read: 'They hated knowledge, and did not choose the fear of the Lord; they would none of my counsel; they despised all my reproof; therefore shall they eat the fruit of their own way.' In the parable of the prodigal son we have the same principle operating; I am sure that the Father had reasoned with his son many times, had pleaded with him, had even argued with him; but in the end he let him go. If the younger son was not prepared to learn by precept that life under the authority of His Father was best, then he would have to learn that it was so by bitter experience in the far country.

So we need to hold in view two things. The first is what I have called *the intention of God.* If we take these words as referring to the action that God was intending to take, we have to think through to the objective behind that intention. If God was going to withdraw the tokens of His grace and favour, it was surely so that, discovering the tragic gap which that action would cause, Ephraim would then turn back in penitence and seek the will of God again. What God was in effect saying was this: 'If you don't want Me, then you need not have me, and then and only then will you discover just how much I have been doing for you.'

Is this not just what so often we do with a wilful and stubborn child? It may be a child who, in spite of many warnings, plays with a box of matches. In the end the child is left to strike a match and in doing so burns a finger or a hand. The pain of that experience is, in the end, the only way in which the child will learn that the parents prohibition was a good and wise one. Or there may be a child who insists on running away. The mother gets tired of chasing after the little rebel, so finally lets the child run on. When the child turns round, Mummy is not there. Immediately panic sets in and the child returns. So in the following chapter we read in Hosea 5.6: 'They shall seek the Lord . . . but they shall not find Him, He hath withdrawn Himself from them.'

The intention of God is not to forsake finally and for ever, but to instruct a disobedient people who would not learn any other way than through the discipline of withdrawal. It is so sometimes with the individual still. There will be no sound of His voice, no sense of His presence, no restraint by His Spirit, and suddenly the soul finds itself unexpectedly and frighteningly alone.

But if we take these words as referring to the action that Judah was being urged to take, then we face another warning not so much to do with the intention of God as with *the infection of sin*. God was possibly telling Judah to keep clear of Ephraim in her rebellious state, in case that same spirit of rebellion might begin to affect the loyalty of Judah. The discipline of withdrawal may not only be experienced through a loss of fellowship with God, but also through a loss of fellowship with God's people! All I do know is that if we are out of harmony with the will of God, then we are almost certainly going to find ourselves out of harmony with those who are seeking to do that will. We will find ourselves ill at ease in their company, and they may very well find themselves to be ill at ease in ours. There is nothing more hurtful than this, when we have known such fellowship both with God and with our fellow believers, suddenly to find that we are, as it were, out in the cold.

Our study however ends on a happy note when finally we look at what I have called –

A DISCOVERY THAT WAS BLESSED. At the end of the fifth chapter we hear God saying through His prophet, 'In their affliction they will seek me early saying, Come let us return to the Lord for He hath torn and He will heal, He hath smitten and He will bind us up.' The discipline of withdrawal was planned to lead to this discovery; there was nothing revengeful about it, but something remedial. So we find at the end of all their experience a blending of two things.

There was *the sadness they would know*. With the presence of God no longer desired and no longer heeded, they would be left to their own devices. Their experience would be like that of the prodigal son who in a sense had to go into the far country before he could come to himself. He had thought himself wise, and had been proved a fool; he had thought he would be free, but he found that he had become a slave. He was sure that he would find happiness away from the authority of his father, but he had become utterly miserable. He had thought that he would find wealth, but he had become a pauper. He had thought that he would make a great success of life, instead he had proved he was an utter failure.

It was in a very similar way that the woman our Lord met at the well at Sychar came to her senses. She had sought satisfaction in a licentious living, in gratifying her senses, in getting her own way in everything. Our Lord challenged her: 'Whosoever drinketh of this water shall thirst again', living that kind of life would bring only momentary and passing satisfaction. Life would then become empty again.

God has made the world and man that way. Man was made for God and can never find true happiness away from Him. The good book says, 'Thou hast created all things and for Thy pleasure they are and were created.' As the fish have been made for the sea, as the flowers have been made for the sun, and the birds have been made for the air, so man has been made for God. 'Thou has made us for Thyself, and our hearts are restless until they find their rest in Thee.' No truer words than these were ever penned by man! When man leaves God out of his living, he is stepping out of his natural and intended environment and element. When man thinks that he can live without reference to God, he is heading for disaster.

But the sadness they would find was intended to lead to *the gladness they would find*. In Hosea 14.4 we read these wonderful words of hope and healing: 'I will heal their backsliding, I will love them freely, for mine anger is turned away. . . Ephraim shall say, "What have I any more to do with idols?"' 'In their affliction they will seek me early.' It was when the prodigal son found himself in the gutter that he came to himself and then came to his father. The woman at the well at Sychar, who was told by her Lord that the water with which she had been trying to quench her thirst, would never do that, was told by that same Lord that there was another water from another well. 'Whosoever drinketh of the water that I shall give him shall never thirst, but the water that I shall give him shall be in him, a well of water springing up into everlasting life.'

Somewhere or other in my reading I read of a girl who had been terribly injured in a car smash. She was brought into hospital but there was nothing that could be done to save her life. She had turned her back upon God and now the life that she had chosen to live was about to end. She was entrusted to the care of a Christian nurse who was told, 'She won't last the night'. The nurse sat by her bed and watched and prayed. Suddenly the girl's eyes opened and the girl spoke, 'Can God love anyone like me?' was her question. Simply the Christian nurse told her of God's love for sinners. The eyes closed again and a few minutes later the girl's breathing ceased, but the serenity that had come into her face which could be seen through the bandages was that of a soul that had at last found peace.

By why wait until we are dying to find that peace? Someone said about the two thieves who were crucified with Christ, 'One was saved that none might despair, but only one that none might presume.' But what a tragic loss when we lose all that God could mean to us in life and through us for others, while all the time our lives can be lived daily in simple obedience to the will of God, that will of God which Paul describes as 'good, perfect and acceptable'.

18

JOEL: BACK MOVES

'I will restore unto you the years that the locust hath eaten.'
(Joel 2.25).

Some years ago, a world-famous preacher and still more
famous writer was introduced to the General Assembly of
the Church of Scotland as the man whose books were on all
our bookshelves and whose illustrations were in all our
sermons. His name was, of course, Dr. F. W. Boreham,
whose ministries were largely located down under in New
Zealand, in Tasmania and in Australia.

In his book, *The Luggage of Life*, Dr. Boreham has a
chapter titled, 'Back Moves'. He begins by recalling an
incident that happened to him in his own home. He was
sitting reading by the fireside. His children were playing a
game at the table. Suddenly the quietness was broken by
one of the children calling out sharply, 'You can't do that.
There are no back moves.' No back moves? Strange as it
may seem, the doctor had not read much further on in his
book, when he came across this sentence. It read: 'The
unseen opponent in the great game of life will allow no back
moves and make us pay in full for every blunder.' The
words were the words of Huxley.

No back moves? Was the child right? Was Huxley right?
Dr. Boreham let the book lie as he meditated and thought
over the question.

For an answer, let us turn to the Word of God for our
guidance and to another equally famous preacher, the
great Doctor Alexander Whyte of Free St. George's
Church, Edinburgh, who for more than forty years filled
that pulpit with distinction, a man who had been born in

poverty, and whose parents were never married! Dr. Whyte once preached a sermon on our text which he called, 'The Locust-eaten Past'. And with his help as well, let us allow the light of God's truth to shine into our hearts as we seek to face the challenge of the words of the child, of the words of the philosopher, and of the words of our own hearts. Are there no back moves in life? Listen to our text again. God says, 'I will restore unto you the years that the locust hath eaten.'

The prophet bases his words upon an experience only too familiar in Eastern lands. He was picturing the utter devastation wrought by the advent of a swarm of locusts. Scholars are not sure as to what it is that the prophet refers. Was he referring to an historical event that had already happened? Or, are his words a symbolical prophecy describing the advent of the armed might of some foreign power and the devastation that would be wrought in the land? Or was it a wholly spiritual message with an application to a much deeper tragedy? Dr. Whyte quotes from Dr. Pusey, one of the great commentators of a former generation, pointing out that Pusey takes the last as being the right interpretation of the words of the prophet. He comments, 'It is clear to me now that these are not literal locusts. There is something here far worse than any locusts. There is some dark riddle of human misery here that neither our learned naturalists nor our Eastern travellers know anything about. But I think that I know now. Joel's locusts are not so far away as Arabia or Palestine. For all Joel's locusts, in all their kinds, and in all their devastation are in my own heart.' And Dr. Whyte, that prince of preachers, adds his own terse comment, 'There is only one thing on the face of the whole earth that this can be – this is sin.'

That being so, let us bring our lives into the light of this portion of God's Word and see if we can find God's answer to the cry of the child and to the claim of the philosopher. 'There are no back moves.' Are they right or are they wrong? What does God's Word mean when it says in God's Name, 'I will restore unto you the years that the locust hath eaten'?

Let us note three things. We have to note that here we have –

THE TARGET FOR SIN'S ATTACK. What a description we have here of the advancing hordes in Chapter 2, verses 1-11! But where is the attack launched? At what target? The target is identified in Chapter 2, verse 3 where we read: 'The land is as the Garden of Eden before them.' I wonder if there are some people reading these words whose reaction already is, 'But I don't know anything of such attacks of the enemy of souls. The thrust of the words of this prophecy to me are meaningless.' To which the only reply would seem to me to be to remind such readers that there are some places that the locust hordes never touch! They are not interested in attacking deserts. They attack where 'the land is as of the Garden of Eden before them'. On land like that, on lives like that, they will descend in their millions, blacking out the light even of the sun itself.

What, then, are the characteristics of the life that is 'as the Garden of Eden', the life that will also be the target for sin's attack? There were two things found distinctively by our first parents in the Garden of Eden. The first was *their experience of the presence of God*. We read in Genesis 3.8 that 'the Lord God, walked in the Garden in the cool of the day'. Show me a life into which the living Christ has come to dwell by His Spirit – a life which has known and enjoyed the wonder of fellowship with God, where the blessedness of communion with God over His Word, in the daily walk, in the fellowship of His people, where all this has been a real and abiding experience – show me such a life and you will show me a life that is as the Garden of Eden, a life that is the target of sin's attack.

On the other hand, show me a life that knows nothing of this; where the Book is never read; where the voice of prayer is never heard; show me a life that has never trod the Emmaus Road and never experienced the wonder of the third Presence emerging out of the shadows to fall in step along the dusty, stony way; show me a life like that and you show me a life that the locust hordes pass by. Yes, the

Garden of Eden life is the life marked by an experience of the presence of the living God.

But it is also surrounded by *the evidence of the power of God*. In Genesis 2.8, we are told, 'The Lord God planted the Garden.' The whole environment in which they lived bore witness to the creative power of God.

But others have lived in an environment like that, where the evidence of God's creative power in a new creation has been equally clear. They have known it in their own lives; we have seen and known it in ours. We have seen God's power at work in other lives, too. Maybe we have seen God's power at work through our own witness, through our own prayers. We have seen what God can do and we know what God has done.

We have seen so much of the loveliness of the recreative work of God, that we could no more deny the reality of that than of our own existence. Show me such a life and you will show me a life that is 'as the Garden of Eden', and that is the target for sin's attack. The locust hordes will seek out such a life to destroy it.

But show me a life that knows nothing of this; a life that is content with the formality of religion with a meaningless membership of the Church; with a dead orthodoxy in what it believes, that knows nothing of the power of the living God working in and working through it. Show me a life that knows nothing of the burden of the world's needs; nothing of the responsibilities of Christian living and witnessing and prayer. Show me such a life and you show me a life that the locust hordes will pass by.

So, we have identified the target for sin's attack. The Garden of Eden life with its experience of the presence of God and with its evidence of the power of God.

But we have something more here, we have what I have called –

THE TRAGEDY OF SIN'S ADVENT. Joel 2.3 tells us that, 'the land before them is as of the Garden of Eden and behind them the desolate wilderness' – a desolate wilderness! And this, let us note, is not simply an historical fact, this is a spiritual fact. The locust hordes of sin can reduce the garden to a wilderness.

Let us note two things; first of all, *how severe is the devastation wrought*. Chapter 2, v.3, tells us, 'Nothing shall escape.' Can there be any greater tragedy spiritually than this? To see a life that has once been like a Garden of Eden turned into a desolate wilderness in which nothing has escaped; a life so spiritually devastated that everything that once was, would seem as if it had never been!

I remember turning the pages of my Bible one evening when I was with my young people in one of my churches. The pages of my Bible were marked. Verses were underlined. Notes had been made in the margin. Suddenly the voice of one of my Sunday-School children looking over my shoulder interrupted. 'My Daddy's Bible is just like that,' she said. Maybe it was like that, but her Daddy was seldom if ever seen in church now! And I wondered how old the ink was in his Bible, marked like mine.

The tragedy of sin's advent is in the severity of the devastation wrought. 'Nothing has escaped.' Our Bible hasn't escaped. It is neglected now. And, if, occasionally it is picked up, God's voice seems seldom, if ever, to be heard. Our prayer life has not escaped. Our private prayer life has dwindled away until it has almost ceased to be. And for going to the prayer-meeting that once we went to, we are never seen there now. Our witness for Christ has not escaped. There was a time when there was a freshness about it and we were willing to speak and to share with others the faith that we had found, and to speak of the Saviour who had come to mean everything to us. But we seldom, if ever, speak of Christ now. Not for a long time. Our home has not escaped. At one time it was a place where, somehow or other, the sense of God's presence seemed to mean much to us all. But now things are different; where once there seemed to be sunlight and spiritual sensitivity, there is darkness. Our giving hasn't escaped, either. Once we gave so faithfully, so regularly, so generously, but not now. Our children haven't escaped. Isn't this a tragic reality in life as we know it? The tragedy of sin's advent. The land that before them was like the Garden of Eden, behind them has become a desolate wilderness.

How severe is the devastation! And *how sustained is the devastation*! Our text speaks of 'the years that the locust hath eaten'. This can have one of two meanings, or possibly both. It may mean that year after year the locust hordes have come and wrought havoc in the land and in the soul. Or, that what they had destroyed was the fruit of years of toil. Either or both can be true.

Have we not known a life that was once as the Garden of Eden remain a desolate spiritual wilderness for years? Have we not seen the fruit of years of devotion and dedication swept away almost in a moment – a garden today, a wilderness tomorrow. The tragedy of sin's advent. The target for sin's attack and the tragedy of sin's advent. But what more? Is there no hope? Are there no back moves? What does our text say? Surely the words here do speak of hope. Listen again to what God says. 'I will restore unto you the years that the locust hath eaten'.

Surely this speaks of something else, of something wonderfully different, of something completely, miraculously Divine. For God is saying, 'I will'. We thought of the target of sin's attack, we have looked at the tragedy of sin's advent, now let us examine what we find here. I have called it –

THE TRIUMPH OF SIN'S ARREST. 'I will restore unto you.' There it is God speaking and He is speaking to us. 'I will restore,' He says, 'to you,' He says, 'the years that the locusts have eaten.' Surely there is hope then. Did another prophet not say something about a vessel that was marred in the hand of the potter? But it wasn't thrown away, was it? It was made again another vessel as seemed good to the potter to make. And there is no hint in the Bible account we find in Jeremiah, Chapter 18, that the new vessel was any less beautiful, any less useful than the first one the potter had been making. Are there, then, no back moves or is it possible after all? Can the past somehow be regained? Can the power of sin be broken? Yes, it can. Of course it can when God says, 'I will'.

I want us to note *the prayer that God was waiting to hear*. In Chapter 2, verses 12-17, it is made absolutely plain that if we are going to see what God can do, then we must want it. We must ask. We must turn from our sin and turn to Him with all our heart. What a word this is! 'Therefore, also now, saith the Lord, turn ye even to me with all your hearts and with fasting and weeping and with mourning and rend your heart and not your garments and turn unto the Lord your God for He is gracious and merciful; slow to anger and of great kindness and repenteth Him of the evil. Who knoweth if he will return and repent and leave a blessing behind him.' So we must turn. We must repent. We must seek and we will find the prayer that God is waiting to hear. Is that prayer our prayer? Do we really want to see the years that the locusts have eaten restored?

The prayer that God is waiting to hear, and what else do we find? *The power that God is willing to give*. To do what? What He said He would do. And that is to restore the years that the locusts have eaten. And if you ask me, 'How can God do that?', I think that God can do it in two ways. The first is by the profusion of the harvest He will now secure in our lives. You see, it doesn't matter so much how long we live, as how we live. The poor harvests of many years can be greatly exceeded by the abundant harvest of a few. Yes, God can do it by the profusion of the harvest.

God can also do it by the perfection of the fruit. God can bring a new quality into our lives, an attractiveness, a Christlikeness, a usefulness that was not there before. And the fruitfulness that might have been and was not, can be exceeded in the mercy of God both in the profusion of the harvest and in the perfection of the fruit in the years that God will restore to us.

Some of us may live long lives; many years, but there is not all that much harvest and fruit to be seen. Others live a short life for a few years and the harvest is bountiful beyond all calculations. One of the saintliest men who ever was a minister in Scotland and whose name is still fragrant in the

158

memory of the Christian Church was Robert Murray McCheyne of St. Peter's Church, Dundee. He died before he was thirty! What an abundant harvest there was in his short life!

God can do a miracle still today. So if the devil comes and tells you there are no back moves, he is telling a lie. For with God, the God of miracles, the God of the impossible, there are back moves. There can be a profusion of the harvest in the soul of a man and a perfection of the fruit of the spirit in the life of a man. And, although the life that was like the Garden of Eden, and has become a wilderness, is a wilderness indeed, the reverse can happen in the life that is a wilderness, a desert. It can become a Garden of Eden again.

May that life be yours and mine to the glory and praise of our God.

19

ZECHARIAH: THE SERVANT OF GOD AND THE SPIRIT OF GOD

'Not by might, nor by power, but by my Spirit, saith the Lord' (Zechariah 4.6).

There is an old saying which describes the connection between the Old and the New Testaments, which says, 'The Old is by the New explained, the New is in the Old contained.' This statement in the book of Zechariah sounds like two verses at least in the New Testament. In John 15.5 our Lord warns his disciples, 'Without Me ye can do nothing' and again in Luke 24.49 He tells them, 'Tarry ye in the city of Jerusalem until ye be endued with power from on high.' Matching those words spoken on the Mount of the Ascension and recorded in Acts 1.8, 'Ye shall receive power after that the Holy Ghost is come upon you and ye shall be witnesses unto Me . . . unto the uttermost parts of the earth.' Power is thus promised, but the source of that power is most clearly indicated as not being in man but in the person of the Spirit of God. It is this connection between the servant of God and the Spirit of God, which is made so much more explicit in the New Testament, that we are to examine now.

There are four important considerations to be kept in mind, if the Holy Spirit is going to be free to do His work in and through the servant of God. The servant must take heed as to the nature of –

THE MESSAGE ON HIS LIPS. The reason for this is quite simple and obvious. The Holy Spirit is 'the Spirit of truth' (John 16.13); this implies surely that the Spirit of God is not going to set His seal upon a message that is not in harmony with the truth of God as revealed in the Word of God.

Then *the matter of the message* is important. The moment I depart from the truth of the Word of God, I depart from the co-operation of the Spirit of God. When Paul took his farewell of the elders at Ephesus, he was at pains to point out that he had not failed to 'declare unto them *the whole counsel of God*'. So the message must cover 'the whole counsel of God'. The tragedy of a great deal of so-called evangelical preaching is that there is a concentration upon the way **in** to the kingdom, through what Christ has done for us on the Cross, and of course we must begin there, but we dare not stop there! The gospel, which is good news, has to do not simply with the way in but with the way *on*! That is good news too, the good news not simply of a new relationship with God, but of new resources in Christ. As I mentioned earlier, there are varying kinds of sermons, some are all door and no house, others are all house and no door, and yet others have both door and house, but they have no windows! If evangelicals concentrate sometimes upon the door and give no indication of the house into which the door opens, the so-called liberals concentrate upon the house and give no indication at all as to how that house can be entered at all! Was it not the great Dr. Alexander Whyte who gave the counsel to one of his assistants, 'Never forget to tell them "how".'

But not only is the matter of the message important, but *the manner of the messenger*. The messenger can as much misrepresent his Master not by **what** He says, but **how** he says it. We read in John 1.14 how John says that when the Word became flesh and dwelt among men, 'We beheld His glory, the glory as of the only begotten of the Father full of grace and truth.' There is much so-called evangelical preaching which may be packed full of truth, but may be totally destitute of grace! I remember once passing a preacher in one of the side streets of London. He had a captive audience, captive, that is, if they wanted to get their shopping done at the market stalls which lined the road. But as I listened to him while he hammered the people and shouted his message, I found myself asking, 'Would Jesus

Christ ever have spoken like that?' and the answer was, 'No, He never would!' Sometimes it is not that we are hard, but so serious as to be excessively dull! It was that well-known preacher, minister of Madison Avenue Presbyterian Church in New York, Dr. David H. C. Read, who once said, 'the worst sin is dullness'!

I recall on one occasion when I had been preaching in a church where the ministry was as true to the Word of God as it could have been, after the service a fine, godly elder came up to me with his comment, 'We have seen something in the pulpit today that we haven't seen for years!' When I asked him rather wonderingly what that might have been, he replied, 'A smile'! The good news had been preached without ever a smile! How utterly heretical some of our so-called faithful preaching can be because it misrepresents our Master not through any fault in **what** we say, but in **how** we say it. So the message on my lips is important if the Spirit of Truth is going to add His 'Amen' to the words I say, both in the matter of the message and in the manner of the messenger.

Then there is another consideration that is as important and that concerns –

THE MOTIVE IN HIS HEART, if the servant of God is going to be blessed with the help of the Spirit of God. We need then to turn to our Bibles to find out what are the motivating purposes in the mind of the Spirit of God. We are told of two and these must be heeded by the servant of God.

What then are *the purposes of the Spirit of God*? Christ Himself tells of two purposes that are in a sense one. In John 16.14 we read that 'He will glorify Me' and in John 15.26, 'He shall testify of Me'. So the over-ruling purpose of the Spirit of God is to make the Saviour known, and to glorify the Saviour before men. His purpose is not to glorify the preacher or the messenger. I remember hearing of one young minister who told his congregation that the best thing he had to offer to them was himself! I found myself thinking of the words of St. Paul, 'we preach not ourselves,

162

but Christ Jesus'. If the work of the Holy Spirit is to glorify Christ, we do well to ask ourselves what that means? Surely it means, at least, that the purposes of God in sending Christ to be the saviour of the world should be realised in the lives of others, that He should be trusted and obeyed. There is a great deal of talk in some religious circles today which seeks to denigrate preaching and to exalt worship. But what is worship? Worship surely means giving a person His worth in our lives! If that be so, then preaching is essential to worship! Indeed, I would go so far as to say that the highest point in worship, when the Word of God is faithfully preached, comes at the end of the sermon, in the responsive and obedient reaction of the worshipper to the Word of God and through the Word of God to a God whom the hearer has come to know better, and to Whose will the hearer is now more rightly related!

This immediately suggests another question and that is, what then are *the perils for the servant of God*? The answer is pretty clear. The perils centre round the temptations that have to do with wanting people to think well of us, rather than to think well of our Saviour, to court popularity, rather than fidelity, and in doing that to compromise our message, to water down the truth of God lest we may cause offence to our friends or to the members of the Church! How many a young man has set out to serve his God, whether it be in the ministry or as a Christian layman, to find this subtle temptation creeping up up on him, to adjust what he has to say and how he is going to live to the wishes and to the standards of the ungodly society in which he finds himself, or even to the standards of a worldly Church!

There is another consideration to be kept in mind if the servant of God is to be sure of the blessing of the Spirit of God, and that concerns –

THE METHODS IN HIS WORK. When we turn to the Bible we find that people are God's method – God reaches men through men! E. M. Bounds, in his well-known book, *Power Through Prayer*, begins by stressing this; he writes: 'God's plan is to make much of a man, far more of him than of anything else, men are God's method. The Church is looking for better methods; God is looking for better men.' Later on he writes: 'What the Church needs today is . . . men whom the Holy Ghost can use, men of prayer, men mighty in prayer.'

If this be so, then two issues are raised, and the first involves this, that *the responsibility for the work must be shared by all*; the immensity of the task demands this, as well as the diversity of gifts. It is going to take all of the Church to reach all of the world and thus fulfil the command of Christ. The gifts may be natural gifts that God wants to use, such as our differing but sanctified personalities; the gifts may be spiritual gifts, those gifts that the Holy Spirit allocates at His own will, giving different gifts to different people. The tragedy is that so much of the activity of the Church, if activity there be, is left to the vicar or the curate, to the pastor or the deacons, to the minister or the elders. But the Bible says that the Church, the whole Church, is the body of Christ, and the whole body is the instrument through which the wishes of the head, who is Christ, are put into effect. Think of the numbers of people whom each member is in touch with throughout any given week, and then add them all together and see what an immense opportunity these numbers constitute. Think of the area of known need that is then opened up to the influence of the witness and of the prayers of the total body of the Church. Wars are not fought by the generals and commanders-in-chief, but by all the ranks at all levels, not forgetting those who toil and sweat in the factories behind the scenes in the home country to provide the needful supplies of every kind!

The other issue that is involved is that not only must the responsibility for the work be shared, but also that *a flexibility in the work must be shown by all*! Not only do different people have different gifts, but those to whom we are to take the gospel have different needs, and so various keys will be needed to open the doors into various hearts. It is significant how in the Scriptures the needs that brought men and women to Christ were infinitely varied and what

He had to say to them when they came thus was different in every case. Of course everything that is done must be done under the guidance of the Holy Spirit, everything that is done will be soaked in prayer, but everything that is done will not be the same in every case. Here it may be an invitation, not to church first of all, but to somebody's home! What will open the door to someone's lonely heart will not be a tract, but some of some Christian's time, a much more costly thing to give! The Church may have to accept that there does come a time in the life of most cities when if a big impact is to be made then it will require what is called in war a major offensive, when after long and careful preparation a special effort is made in which all the Churches work together to reach the masses who never darken the door of their churches. Someone has made the comment that he sees no place in Scripture for, what he called, this organised evangelism, but I see no place in Scripture for organised preaching of the word, something for which the same man is well-known, nor for organised worship! The only scripture that I have that tells me anything says, that 'All things [and that presumably includes evangelism] are to be done decently and in order.'

When our Lord spoke of the Holy Spirit to Nicodemus, He likened the movement of the Holy Spirit to the wind, so often quite unexpected and unpredictable in the direction from which it will come. If we believe in the sovereignty of God at all, we must surely allow Him to be free to work outside the narrow confines of our own ideas and traditions. The witness of history confirms that when God does move in power it is so often through the most unexpected and most unlikely channels, and that when He does thus move He blows all our preconceived ideas to smithereens!

We have thought of the message on the lips of the servant, and then finally we must consider –

THE MANNER OF THE LIFE OF THE SERVANT.
The Holy Spirit is called the Spirit of God. Therefore the manner of the life of the servant of God must correspond to the life of the Spirit of God if the Spirit is going to set his

seal of approval on that work! The New Testament revelation of the nature of God as revealed in Jesus Christ is twofold. We are told that God is light, and that God is love.

The God Who is light is the God of the Bible. Light speaks of two things: it speaks of truth or knowledge, and it speaks of holiness. Darkness in the Bible is the darkness either of ignorance or sinfulness. If we consider holiness, we find that there is a negative side to holiness, so there are some things that can have no place in the life of the servant of God, because they are sinful. But there is also a positive side to holiness, so there are things that will have a place in the life and character of the servant of God. They will be produced in him, through the presence and power of the Spirit Who is dwelling in him. But not only will his life be marked by holiness, it will be marked by knowledge and truth. His life will be lived in the light of the truth as it is in Christ Jesus.

The God Who is love is the God of the Bible. While the light will be reflected, the love will be revealed. I wonder how many Christians have ever faced up to the challenge and implications of the words of the risen Christ in the upper room when He said to his disciples, 'As the Father hath sent me, even so send I you.' The Father sent the Son to redeem mankind, and to renew mankind, but also to reveal Himself to mankind. So that Christ was able to say, 'He that hath seen Me hath seen the Father.' The logical conclusion of the words of Christ mean then that we too are to share in the redeeming, renewing and revealing ministry of Christ. We are therefore expected to show the caring love and compassion of God for man in his great need. The Church should be the caring community, revealing God's caring love for the whole man. Men ought to be able to say of the servants of God, 'he that hath seen them hath seen the Christ'.

We have considered the four-fold relationship between the servant of God and the Spirit of God. What a relationship it is – and what a responsibility! Let us never forget the words of the prophet who said it is 'not by might, nor by power, but by my Spirit, saith the Lord!'

20

MALACHI: LIFE'S REFINING FIRES

'And he shall sit as a refiner and purifier of silver'
(Malachi 3.3).

The verse upon which I want us to base our thinking comes from the last book of the Old Testament, the book of the Prophet Malachi. Here we have this prophetic description of the relationship between God and His people. In Chapter 3, verses 3 and 4, we read: 'And he shall sit as a refiner and purifier of silver. And he shall purify the sons of Levi and purge them as gold and silver that they may offer unto the Lord their offering in righteousness. Then shall the offering of Judah and Jerusalem be pleasant unto the Lord as in the days of old.'

I want to link that verse with a similar one in the New Testament. In 1 Peter 1.6-7 Peter, writing of the trials through which the Christians were passing, speaks in this way. He speaks of 'The trial of your faith being much more precious than of gold that perisheth, though it be tried with fire, might be found unto praise and honour and glory at the appearing of Jesus Christ.'

Our theme, then, concerns what I have called, 'Life's Refining Fires'. Those of us who know our Bibles, know that we have many many different pictures presented to us in the Word of God that are designed to illustrate the nature of the relationship between God and His people. Indeed, we might, if we had chosen, have taken as our title, 'How God Deals With His Own'. We are familiar with some of the pictures more than others – the picture of the Father and his child. How basic and blessed that relationship is to those who have been born again into the family of

God! We are even more familiar from our childhood of the pattern of the Shepherd and the sheep. Then there is the picture of the Vine-dresser and the vine, or of the Potter and the clay, or of the Bridegroom and the bride. To me they are all different pictures, each emphasising a different aspect of the relationship between God and His own.

I wonder, though, how much thought we have given to this prophetic picture in Malachi which describes the relationship in these words, that he, 'shall sit as a refiner and purifier of silver'. Here we have the picture of how God deals with His own as that of a refiner purifying the silver. When I found myself studying this, I wished that I could have got into touch with one of my former church members who was a craftsman in the art of silver and gold. I would have liked to examine with him exactly what he felt would be the implications of this passage. But with such knowledge as I might have it seemed to me that there are three things with which we have to reckon as we consider how God deals with His own.

First of all, we can note –

THE MOTIVATION IN THE REFINER'S HEART.
The refiner and purifier of silver has a concern about what is happening to the metal, which I believe God shares with what is happening to His people. Let us then consider *the purpose on which the refiner's mind is resolved*. The purpose in refining the silver is quite obviously the purity of the silver or the gold with which he is working, to get rid of the impurities in the metal that would spoil the work on which he would exert and demonstrate his skills. Those of us who have been to Eastern countries know how widely displayed is the work of the silversmith or goldsmith. Most of us will have come back with some evidences of their skill in our pockets or handbags. But I wonder how far we are prepared to accept the fact that the purpose of God for our lives is that they should be holy. That is, that they should be set apart both outwardly and inwardly, both in conduct and in character, from all that is inconsistent with the mind of

God and unworthy of the Name of God. The purpose on which the refiner's mind is resolved is the purity of the silver or the gold. So we read in the Bible, 'As he which hath called you is holy, so be ye holy in all manner of conversation; (that is, in all your conduct) because it is written, "Be ye holy, for I am holy".'

I remember hearing of a schoolboy who went to church and when he got back his mother asked him what the preacher had talked about. The boy said, 'He talked about God and sin'. His mother said, 'And what did he have to say about sin?' The boy replied, 'Well, as far as I could make out, he said that God was against it.' And isn't this true? Do you remember how Paul wrote to the Ephesian church in Ephesians 5.25? He speaks of the love of Christ for the Church and that Christ gave Himself for the Church, 'That he might present it unto himself not having spot or wrinkle or any such thing but that it should be holy and without blemish.' Or, you might recall these tremendous words in the Epistle to the Hebrews, which, some think, might have been dictated by Paul and then interpreted and written down by the hand of Luke. 'Thy throne, Oh God, is for ever and ever. A sceptre of righteousness is a sceptre of Thy Kingdom. Thou hast loved righteousness and hated iniquity.'

I wonder what God has to say about what we call our modern permissive society which seems to be willing to permit almost anything. As I read my Bible I find that there is one great intolerance in the heart and mind of God and that is that God is utterly intolerant of sin! But it is the intolerance of love. It is not a harsh intolerance; it is a heartbroken intolerance. Here we have love's intolerance of anything unworthy in the lives of those it loves, and also we have love's insistence on everything that is worthy in the life of those it loves. The purpose, then, on which the refiner's mind is resolved is the purity of the silver.

We see, also – *the process by which the refiner's aim is achieved*. It is through a refining by fire. The metal is placed in the crucible above the flame so that the impurities may first of all be revealed in the molten mass and then removed. This is exactly what Peter is referring to in 1 Peter 1.6-7, where he writes of the way in which, 'Now for a season, if need be, ye are in heaviness through manifold temptations: that the trial of your faith, being much more precious than of gold that perisheth, though it be tried with fire, might be found unto praise and honour and glory at the appearing of Jesus Christ.'

Fire speaks surely of suffering, of trials, of affliction, not necessarily physical; more often, maybe, mental and sometimes social, sometimes imposed at the hands of men; sometimes designed and permitted by the love of God; sometimes they may arise out of our own waywardness, but always intended and shaped to fulfil the one object, to reveal the unworthy facets of our life and character so that they may, then, with our glad consent, be dealt with by God.

This, then, surely is the motivation in the refiner's heart and suggests right away that being a Christian can well become a most uncomfortable way of life. And, in one sense, that is precisely what it is. I wonder how often you and I are made to feel uncomfortable in our Christian experience. I remember a lady saying once to me that whenever she went to church when I preached, she was made to feel such a sinner. Well, all that I could say was that it was a sinner that was doing the preaching. And that it was not the preacher who made her feel a sinner, for that is surely simply the work of the Spirit of God! Yes, the motivation in the refiner's heart is to get rid of everything in your life and mine which is unworthy and the process is the process of trial and affliction, of pressure and suffering.

Now, this is disturbing, but it is quite biblical. And far from being dismayed if I am made to feel uncomfortable under the preaching of the Word, I should be delighted. Because it means, simply, that God is dealing with me. The people who should be most disturbed if they come into a service where the Word of God is faithfully proclaimed are the people who are the least disturbed. I would hate to bring my life into the light of the Word of God and go out smug and satisfied and complacent. The standards of God are infinitely higher than the standards of men. And I should expect that God would have something to say to me and I should be so delighted when He does, for it means that the refiner is at work in my life.

The second thought that came to me had to do with what I called –

THE REGULATION BY THE REFINER'S HAND. I want to note how Malachi speaks of the coming Redeemer as a refiner and purifier of silver and describes Him in this way: 'He shall sit as a refiner and purifier of silver.' In other words, He is on the job and He is on the job all the time. This suggests, first of all, *how watchful He is*.

How watchful! The picture is surely that of a refiner sitting watching the whole process intently. Many years ago when I was quite a young Christian they used to have a convention in Edinburgh which was my home town. It was a kind of miniature Keswick Convention. The meetings were held in a large tent or marquee. Somehow or other that creates a different atmosphere to a meeting held in any other auditorium. The speaker was the late Rev. W. W. Martin who has long since gone to Glory, but whose ministry meant a great deal to me when I used to go to the Keswick Convention as a young man. It was he who spoke of how at one time in his own life he was requiring a piece of metal. If my memory is right, it was a piece of brass and it had to be purified. I remember him describing how the metal was put into the crucible and gradually the scum rose to the surface to be removed. Still the metal was left, still the scum continued to rise and was removed. So the process went on until there was no more impurity left. But the point that came home to me was that the refiner was watching the process.

To me one of the most wonderful truths about the love of God is the knowledge of God. Jesus used to say so often, 'Your Heavenly Father knoweth'. This is one of the most tremendous things on which the heart can rest. Psalm 33.18 tells us that 'God's eye is upon them that fear Him, upon them that trust in His mercy.' Psalm 121.4 tells us that 'He

171

that keepeth Israel shall neither slumber nor sleep.' I wonder how many of us have found our hearts strangely moved when we have heard someone sing the old song, 'His Eye is on the Sparrow and I Know He Watches Me'. Do you find the knowledge that God is watching you disturbing? Or comforting? I find it wonderfully assuring that there is no need to pretend with God. None at all. It's as silly and as stupid to try to cover up before God as it is to try to cover up the flaws in our teeth when we sit in the dentist's chair. All the dentist says is, 'Open your mouth'. And then he will tell you what is wrong. You may have gone to the dentist thinking you had nothing wrong, or maybe hoped you had nothing wrong. But after you have been in the chair for just a few minutes you discover that there are things that need to be put right.

How watchful He is as He treats and tends that metal! I think it would be true to say that not only does God see our suffering and the process going on, but he shares it. You remember the story of the three men in the book of Daniel who were cast into the fiery furnace and how we are told in Daniel 3.24-25 that when they were cast into the fiery furnace, 'Nebuchadnezzar, the king, was astonished, and rose up in haste, and said unto his counsellors, Did we not cast three men bound into the midst of the fire? Now I see four men loose, walking in the midst of the fire, and they have no hurt; and the form of the fourth is like the Son of God.' Love not only sees but shares. Indeed, it is true to say that love suffers even more than the one whose suffering love observes. And when God is dealing with us as a refiner and purifier of silver, He is watching and He is caring, too. He sees, He shares, and He suffers.

How watchful the refiner will be and – *how careful He is*. There is often, if not always, a time factor in almost any process. This is something with which we are familiar: a mother heating the milk for her baby will test it to check whether it is too cold, too hot, or just right. And so she dips her finger in to test it. How careful she is! A wife who is baking a cake for tea knows that if she takes it out too soon, it will be spoiled, or if she leaves it in too long it will be

172

spoiled. How careful she is! There is a time element in almost every process you can think of in life. And so we read exactly the same here. I love the verse in 1 Corinthians 10.13, where we read: 'There hath no temptation or trial taken you but such as is common to man; but God is faithful, who will not suffer you to be tempted above that ye are able to bear.' So God is not only watchful, He is careful too. He doesn't want to hurt. He doesn't want to harm, and so He times the processs precisely. I remember hearing someone commenting on those words about which He said three things. He said that testing or temptation is common to man, controlled by God, and conquerable by us. Note that central phrase, 'it is controlled by God'. There will be a regulation, a careful, watchful regulation of the process by the refiner.

We have noted then, the motivation in the Refiner's heart, and the regulation by the Refiner's hand, and there is just one more thought, as we consider finally –

THE CONSUMMATION OF THE REFINER'S HOPES. When is the process finally completed? Malachi 3.3-4 gives us the answer. 'And He will purge them as gold and silver, that they may offer unto the Lord an offering in righteousness. Then shall the offering of Judah and Jerusalem be pleasant unto the Lord.' The consummation of the refiner's hope – when does that come? It comes *when the silver has been purified*. I must expect, then, in one sense that this experience will continue to be mine throughout my whole life. And, of course, this is true. There are so many unsuspected depths of evil in our fallen nature. There are blemishes in our Christian life of which we may be totally unaware. And so the need will be for them to be revealed. So that then they may be removed by our repentance and His renewing grace. Sometimes we may be tempted to think that spiritually we have really arrived; we have got there! I remember thinking that as a young Christian. It is extraordinary what stupid thoughts you have when you are young. I thought I really was the kind of Christian I ought to be. Have you ever thought that? Don't you believe it. Sometimes when we are tempted to think that way, that we have finally reached the standard of Christian experience that God requires, then God plunges us into new circumstances, subjecting our lives to new strains and stresses and, to our dismay, we find that we still have much to learn and that there is still much more progress to be made.

I have never forgotten how the late Dr. F. B. Meyer, one of the most Godly and saintly ministers who ever preached the Word of God, used to say he could never understand how a minister would ever be guilty of the sin of jealousy. F. B. Meyer was a man to whose ministry people flocked in their thousands. Then one day, when he was speaking at a conference in the United States, he suddenly discovered that the numbers attending his meetings were getting fewer each day. And he heard that the numbers attending another preacher were getting bigger each day. The name of this other preacher was a young man called G. Campbell Morgan, comparatively unknown at that time! For the first time in his life, F. B. Meyer knew the temptation to feel jealous.

Have you ever set out to climb a mountain and after some time thought that you had reached the top? The limit of your vision seemed to be the summit and you thought another hundred yards and you would be there. But when you got there it was only to find that there was another rising hill beyond. When you got to the top of that there was another beyond it. I am not much of a poet, and I don't remember much of the poetry I learned at school, but I seem to remember two lines of one poem, the sentiments of which must have appealed to my nature. The lines read: 'Does the road wind uphill all the way? Yes, to the very end!'

And so the consummation of the refiner's hope will be when the silver has been purified and *when the Saviour has been satisfied*. The key words in Malachi 3 are: 'Pleasant unto the Lord'. Professor William Barclay, whose books I have found helpful, but with whose theology from time to time I have found myself in disagreement, commenting on the words in 1 Peter 1.7, 'that the trial of your faith being much more precious than of gold that perisheth though it be tried with fire may be found unto the praise and honour and glory at the appearing of Jesus Christ', writes: 'Again and again in this life we make our biggest efforts, we do our best work, not for pay and not for profit, but in order to see the light in someone's eyes.' When the Saviour has been satisfied – how true this is! Every child, every parent, knows all about this. Every lover and every sweetheart knows all about it, too. The work, sacrifice, everything is worth while if only the one we love is pleased and delighted and satisfied. In a sense His praise, honour, and glory matter now, but ultimately, they will matter most at His appearing!

I think there is one simple question that every Christian has to ask continually and that is, 'Do we think Jesus Christ is satisfied with our lives as Christians?' I certainly do not think He is and I hope you don't think so, either. If you do think that, then I think you had better get to Glory just as fast as you can, for the only people whom I know, who are satisfied like that, are there! But, 'it will be worth it all when we see Jesus', is the theme of an old song. He shall sit as a refiner and purifier of silver and the consummation of the refiner's hopes comes when the silver has been purified and the Saviour has been satisfied. Someone has suggested that the refiner works on until at last he can see in the molten metal, purified now from every blemish, the reflection of his own face. There is a lovely hymm we sing at the Keswick Convention. The first verse reads:

My Saviour, thou hast offered rest,
Oh, give it then to me;
The rest of ceasing from myself
To find my all in Thee.

But it is the last verse that is the really lovely one. It reads like this:

Work on, then, Lord, till on my soul,
Eternal light shall break;

And in Thy likeness perfected,
I, satisfied, shall wake.

'He shall sit as the refiner and purifier of silver.' We have thought of the motivation in the Refiner's heart, the regulation by the Refiner's hand, the consummation of the Refiner's hope! So may God grant that we may know what it is to know Him not just as Saviour, but as the Refiner, the purifier of silver and gold, for that is what He is!